Stand, Fight, Win

How to Stand Up, Fight Back, and Win Your
Rightful Inheritance

Keith A. Davidson &
Stewart R. Albertson

www.aldavlaw.com

ISBN: 978-1719877756

To my wife, Kristy Davidson,
and my two sons, Weston and Collin.
Without your constant love and support, I could not carry on the important work
I do with our law firm in fighting for the rights of abused beneficiaries.
—Keith A. Davidson

To the best son in the world, Christopher Albertson.
—Stewart R. Albertson

In this world nothing can be said to be certain, except death and taxes.
—Benjamin Franklin

… and inheritance fights.
—Keith A. Davidson

A trust lawsuit is a marathon, not a sprint.
—Stewart R. Albertson

Contents

Introduction

For nearly two decades, we—Keith A. Davidson and Stewart R. Albertson—have fought for the rights of abused trust and will beneficiaries. When we started, we had no idea just how bad this problem was nor how much help people really needed. Over time, however, the true extent of the problem became evident. People from all walks of life have the potential of being abused by a bad trustee or bad executor.

It all starts when a parent creates a revocable living trust (or a will) and names a "trusted" person as trustee or executor. For purposes of this introduction we will focus on trust cases, but all the same can be true for wills too. The problem with revocable living trusts is that they are not administered in court. Trusts were created originally to bypass probate (meaning the passing of assets happens outside of any court supervision), so that the trust administration could be handled privately, and in theory, less expensively than going to court. You see, all wills require probate administration with "probate" referring to the court process where a court oversees the estate administration from start to finish. Trusts don't work like that. Instead, trusts are meant to be private documents, administered outside of court; that makes things easy and less expensive—if only that were true in every case.

There may be a majority of cases where trusts are indeed administered outside of court in a way that is easy and less expensive. But that is not the subject of this book, and not the subject of the authors' law practice either. In fact, we see the worst-case scenarios. And those worst-case scenarios seem to occur everywhere, all the time, to everyone. Maybe abuse does not happen to everyone, but the issues of abuse discussed in this book can happen to anyone.

It all begins with a bad trustee. The trustee is the person who is the legal owner of the trust assets, the trust manager, and the person calling the shots. And when you have a bad trustee, you are bound to have abuse—and lots of it.

How could a trustee be bad? We certainly hate to be the ones to tell you this, but some people are bad. In fact, some people refuse to follow the rules or take their duties and responsibilities seriously. There is an old saying that absolute power corrupts absolutely. Welcome to the world of bad trustees.

In most cases, bad trustees come from private people named to act as trustee. Professional trustees and corporate trustees tend to know and follow the rules more than individual trustees. Plus, the professionals have probably been sued before, and they do not want to lose their own money on a bad trust situation.

Private individuals, on the other hand, have no idea what they are in for because they may never have acted as trustee before. They probably have no idea what their responsibilities are, and they do not realize that they can be held personally liable for the harms they cause to the trust. Yikes! Take our word for it, being a trustee is a thankless job—it comes with all the responsibilities and very little pay—unless it's a bad trustee.

Most bad trustees are siblings of the trust beneficiaries. In fact, sibling trustees can be some of the worst trustees you ever encounter. There's history there; sometimes many years of pain and slights waiting to erupt. What better way to get back at a sibling than to deny them their beneficial interests in a trust.

Out of sibling rivalry, the bad trustee is often born. And bad trustees never seem to see the light until it is too late. All too often a bad trustee will wrongly believe that they can do whatever they like because, as trustee, they are "in charge" of the trust. A bad trustee may even have a lawyer advising them, and still they seem to ignore the obvious truth that they must abide by trust law.

Over the last decade, we (along with attorneys at our firm, Albertson & Davidson, LLP) have represented hundreds of beneficiaries who have to fight against bad trustees. Bad trustees come from all walks of life—rich, poor, educated, uneducated, financially savvy, and financial neophytes. Being a bad trustee is a great social equalizer apparently because it happens across the social spectrum. The one universal truth is that bad trustees cause lasting damage—both financially and emotionally.

So what is an abused beneficiary to do? That's where the following chapters come into play for you. This book will cover the following six main areas where beneficiaries are routinely abused by bad trustees:

1. Abuse involving the distribution of trust assets;

2. Abuse involving the provision of trust financial information or accounting to the beneficiaries;

3. Abuse involving following the trust terms (such as in creating and funding sub-trusts);

4. Abuse involving the diversification of trust assets;

5. Abuse involving the unfair treatment of one or more of the beneficiaries; and

6. Abuse involving a family-owned business.

Each of the six areas is addressed in its own chapter. Each chapter provides a factual scenario to illustrate the typical problem people have with the given abuse area. You will then find recommendations on how we, as trust- and will-focused lawyers, would deal with the problems presented in the factual hypothetical. And finally, you will find a simple-to-understand explanation of the laws that apply to each given topic.

This book is based on California law and is geared towards California trust and will issues. However, beneficiaries located outside of California will find this book helpful if their trust or will matter is governed by California law—many people create trusts or wills in California and then move elsewhere, so California law may still apply. Also, many states use California law, or laws similar to California, in trust or will matters. If you reside outside of California, be sure to consult a local lawyer before taking any action on your trust or will matter.

Our aim with this book is to give you hope that there is a way to combat abuse. First, you should know that you are not alone. Thousands of people suffer from abuse by a bad trustee every day. Our firm, Albertson & Davidson, LLP, has handled hundreds of cases of trustee abuse, and that is just a small fraction of the cases out there. Second, you should know what your rights are so you can understand that (1) you are being abused, and (2) there is a way to fight against abuse. Third, you should know a little something about trust law, so you can ask the right questions and find the right legal help.

Chapter 1

Abuse Involving the Distribution of Trust Assets

In this section we will discuss a trustee's failure to make distribution of trust assets to beneficiaries as required under the terms of the trust.

Let's start with a basic understanding of the trust law we will apply to this problem.

THE BASICS OF CALIFORNIA TRUST DISTRIBUTIONS

Under Probate Code section 16000, a trustee has a duty to administer the trust according to the trust instrument. This duty requires the trustee to distribute trust assets to the beneficiaries as mandated by the trust document.

Sometimes a trustee is granted "absolute" discretion over trust distributions. This means the trustee has the right to make, or not make, any distribution they like. Even when the trustee is granted "absolute" discretion, their power to distribute must be exercised in accordance with fiduciary principles and not in bad faith or in disregard of the purposes of the trust. "Fiduciary principles" essentially means a trustee is supposed to act like a reasonable person would in similar circumstances—in other words: be fair.

Trust Distribution Hypothetical: Brian as Abused Beneficiary

Let's consider a hypothetical situation to demonstrate the problems that arise and the options you have when confronted with a California trustee who fails to distribute trust assets. After the hypothetical, we will discuss trust distributions in more detail.

Brian was the youngest son of a family that had two children. Brian's father, Frank, built four apartment buildings in Los Angeles that had between ten to fifteen apartment units per building. The apartment buildings were built in the 1960s and were owned by Frank until his death in March 2014.

Prior to his death, Frank created a revocable living trust that named his oldest son, Tom, as the successor trustee. The trust terms stated that after all the debts and expenses of the estate were paid, the remaining assets were to be distributed outright to Tom and Brian equally. The trust did not provide any instructions on how to deal with the four apartment buildings.

After Frank's death, Tom quickly took control of the four apartment buildings but used the same property manager that Frank had used for years. Two of the apartment buildings had mortgages against them, and the other two were owned free-and-clear of any mortgages.

Brian assumed that his brother would simply sell the apartment buildings and split the cash between the two beneficiaries. Based on the appraisals obtained by Tom, the total value of all four apartment buildings equaled $14 million. The two mortgages against two of the apartment buildings equaled $4 million total, leaving a net estate of $10 million. After estate taxes and expenses were paid, Brian assumed he would receive close to $4 million.

Tom had other ideas, however, on how to handle the estate. Tom thought that Brian was foolish with his money and would simply spend everything he received from the trust. As a result, Tom decided not to distribute any assets to Brian. Tom also did not want to sell the apartment buildings. Instead, he wanted to continue managing them as his father had and receive the income.

Tom did disclose his plan to Brian. Tom also refused to provide Brian with any financial information (other than the appraisals). Instead, Tom sent $1,000 per month to Brian and told him that was all he was going to receive from the trust. Tom also told Brian that if he hired a lawyer or attempted to challenge anything, then Brian would be disinherited and receive nothing further from the trust.

Brian was frustrated but also afraid to lose his trust share. He believed his brother's threat of being disinherited. Brian never received an accounting or any financial reports, and did not know how to obtain them.

BRIAN'S OPTIONS

It appears that Tom intentionally decided to withhold Brian's share of the trust and prevent him from ever receiving his $4 million. What can Brian do to force a distribution of his inheritance? Here are his options:

1. **File for removal of trustee.** File a petition with the California probate court asking the court to remove Tom as the trustee.

2. **File to obtain a trust accounting.** Demand an accounting in writing, and then file a petition with the California probate court asking the court to order Tom, as the trustee, to account.

3. **File to force a distribution of trust assets.** File a petition for instructions asking the court to force the trustee, Tom, to account.

4. **File for breach of trust against Tom.** File a petition for redress for breach of trust that would seek monetary damages against the trustee, Tom.

5. **Ask Tom to distribute more money without filing in court.** Send an email to Tom asking him to make a proper trust distribution.

OUR EXPERT RECOMMENDATION

Having a bad trustee who refuses to make distributions as required by the trust document is not unusual—it happens more often than you might think. Luckily, in this case Brian is supposed to receive an outright distribution of one-half of the trust estate. There are no restrictions or trusts created for Brian; it is an outright gift. As such, Brian has a right to receive his half of the trust estate within a "reasonable" amount of time.

So why is Tom not honoring Brian's rights? Sounds like Tom is enjoying the status quo. Tom is keeping all of the rents, he does not have to sell any of the properties, and he is keeping money out of Brian's hands. But Tom does not have the right to judge whether or not Brian can properly manage money. If the trust requires an outright distribution, then that must occur. It does not matter if Brian is wasteful with money; half the estate belongs to Brian and Brian must receive it.

Option 2: the first action we at Albertson & Davidson, LLP, would recommend is for Brian to send Tom a written demand for a trust accounting and a trust distribution. A trust accounting refers to a detailed description of all assets received by Tom as trustee, all expenses paid from the trust, all distributions made to beneficiaries, and all assets still held by Tom as trustee. A trust accounting gives the beneficiaries full transparency of trust finances. A trust distribution is the transfer of money or other assets to the beneficiaries. The trustee has sixty days in which to comply and provide a trust accounting. The trust accounting is important because it will allow us to determine how much back rent should go to Brian. Since Tom has been keeping all the rents, that means Tom has failed to give Brian his one-half share of those rents. As a fifty percent beneficiary, Brian is entitled to half of all rents going to back to the date of Frank's death.

Option 3: in most cases, the trustee will refuse to provide an accounting and will also refuse to make a trust distribution. Our next step would be to file a petition for accounting and for a trust distribution. Our goal here would be to have as much money distributed to Brian as possible. We want to get assets into Brian's hands, so Tom cannot continue to abuse the trust assets.

In most cases, the court will agree to order an accounting and also order a trust distribution. Once the accounting is obtained, we can review the information to determine what other damages are due to Brian (such as one-half of the back rent). We can also use the financial information to subpoena records directly from the bank. The bank records will help to substantiate or refute the information provided to us in the trust accounting.

Option 1: the problem with trustee removal is it takes time to remove a trustee. Ultimately, we have to go to trial and present evidence to re-move a trustee. We can ask for temporary suspension of the trustee, which may be a good idea, but removal takes time and costs money. The real goal in this case is to force a total trust distribution to Brian, which can be achieved with Tom as trustee. In fact, we may have more leverage to achieve that with Tom as trustee because the trustee owes Brian substantial fiduciary duties—meaning Tom is under a legal obligation to act reasonably towards Brian even after Brian files his lawsuit in court. Once Tom is removed as trustee, he no longer owes Brian fiduciary duties.

There are some cases where we do bring a removal petition along with the accounting and trust distribution petitions, but we have to evaluate that option carefully. Remember, every petition we bring takes time and money to prosecute, so you may want to spend your time and money on a trust distribution rather than trustee removal.

Option 4: a petition for breach of trust may be possible, but we typically wait until after we receive the trust accounting. The accounting will provide a financial road map that will allow us to find the breaches of fiduciary duties, if there are any. By waiting for the accounting (and the subpoenaed bank information) we can prepare a more targeted petition for breach of trust. This petition can always be filed later after further evidence is located.

Option 5: it never hurts to ask for a trust distribution, but it rarely accomplishes your goal. Many people believe a letter from a lawyer will convince a bad trustee to act appropriately. In our experience, letters rarely work because letters can be ignored. A court lawsuit, with an angry judge staring at the trustee or the trustee's lawyer in court, cannot be ignored. But if you are thinking about emailing the trustee to ask for a distribution, by all means you should do so. And if that works for you, be sure to send us an email to let us know that you are the first person we have ever heard of getting a bad trustee to do the right thing outside of court action.

A Word on No-Contest Clauses

A no-contest clause refers to a provision in a contract that seeks to prevent a contracting party (or beneficiary) from challenging its terms. In Brian's case, Tom's threat that Brian will be disinherited if he hires a lawyer and challenges the trustee is the no-contest clause—and it is completely false. No-contest clauses in California are narrowly enforced, meaning they only apply to challenging the validity of the trust document. Also, no-contest clauses never apply to any action a beneficiary might take to force a trustee to account or to distribute according to the trust terms, or to sue the trustee for breach of trust. As a beneficiary, you will never be disinherited for questioning a trustee or taking actions to force the trustee to act appropriately.

THE LAW OF TRUST DISTRIBUTIONS IN CALIFORNIA

The law of trust distributions is fairly straightforward. Under Probate Code section 16000, the trustee must follow the trust terms. In Leader v. Cords (182 Cal. App. 4th 1588(2010)), the California Appellate Court held that the duty to account is inseparable from the duty to distribute. In other words, a trustee must make a distribution of trust assets in order to meet their duty to administer the trust according to its terms.

The bottom line: the trustee must follow the trust terms. If the trust provides for an outright distribution to a trust beneficiary, then the assets must be distributed outright to that person—no other options are available. Even if the trustee believes the beneficiary is foolish with money or will spend all the money on something bad like drugs, alcohol, or gambling, the distributions must still be made.

If the trust provides for assets to be held in trust and only to make distributions where a need arises, like for health, education, support, or maintenance, then the trustee must make reasonable distributions on that basis. Under no circumstances can a trustee unilaterally decide to keep something that belongs to a beneficiary because the trustee believes it better to do so. The trust terms must be followed. And the overriding guideline is that the trustee act in the best interests of the beneficiary.

The problem is that many private trustees fear making a mistake when distributing large sums to beneficiaries. As a result, trustees would rather hold onto trust assets than make a mistaken distribution. The other fear is that an unknown trust liability will be discovered, like unpaid taxes, an unknown credit card bill, or any other random expense, and the trustee will be responsible for payment after all assets have been distributed. And finally, some private trustees think they can do whatever they like since they, as the trustee, are "in-charge." That's false, but it can be hard to convince a bad trustee of this point.

A Reasonable Trust Reserve

A trust reserve refers to holding money in the trust to pay final trust expenses, such as tax preparation fees, trust taxes, trustee's fees, any debts or bills, and any final attorneys' fees. Every trustee has the right to retain a reasonable trust reserve. The court talks about this point in Leader v. Cords (and there are other cases on the subject as well). Of course, the problem comes down to: what is "reasonable"? If you have a trust with a total value of $10 million, would it be reasonable to withhold a reserve of $1 million? If you have a trust with a total value of $1 million, would it be reasonable to withhold a reserve of $250,000?

That all depends on what is expected to occur after distribution of trust assets. For example, if the trust is subject to a creditor's claim worth $250,000, then a reserve for that amount may be reasonable—even if the claim is disputed. The reserve is reasonable because if the claim is challenged, but ultimately lost, then the trustee would have to pay $250,000. That amount should be set aside until the claim is finalized.

If, however, a trust has no debts or claims against it at all, and the only expected expense is the preparation of a final tax return, then a reserve of $250,000 would be unreasonable for estates of any size. In this case, a reserve of $1,500 may be more than enough to cover any expenses to prepare and file a tax return. Of course, a trustee in this situation will probably ask for a $5,000 reserve to be on the safe side, but that would be more than enough to cover possible expenses.

The reserve, to be reasonable, must be based on a realistic expectation of possible debts and expenses. If a trustee cannot clearly articulate the reason for a given amount in reserve, then the amount they've designated is considered fabricated and should not be allowed.

A REASONABLE TIMEFRAME FOR DISTRIBUTIONS

Trustees always make distributions too slowly, and beneficiaries always expect distributions too soon. This is how trustees and beneficiaries view each other. The law presumes that distributions will be made in a "reasonable" time, but what does that mean?

The amount of time that is "reasonable" can vary greatly from case to case. For example, a distribution that takes place a year after the settlor's death could be reasonable if the trust has real estate (homes, apartments, commercial buildings, etc.) that has to be repaired and then sold. Tax issues or disputed debts can also delay distributions. Alternatively, a trust holding cash with no debts should make distributions within a few months.

There are a few statutory or required timeframes to consider as well. For example, under Probate Code section 16061.7, the trustee is required to give notice to all trust beneficiaries after a trust becomes irrevocable, meaning the trust can no longer be amended or changed. The beneficiaries then have 120 days in which to object to the terms of the trust (i.e., to bring a trust contest). After the 120-day period runs, there can be no contest of the trust terms. Therefore, it may be reasonable for a trustee to wait until after the 120-day period expires before making any trust distributions—especially where a trust contest is a concern. In fact, Probate Code section 16061.9(c) specifically allows a trustee to consider this 120-day period in deciding when to make trust distributions.

A trustee also has the right, but not the obligation, to use the creditor's claim procedures provided in Probate Code sections 19000 to 19403. These Probate Code sections allow a trustee to notify all potential creditors of the trust estate and force them to either file a claim or be forever barred from collecting their debt. Once the creditor's claim time period expires, which is four months after it begins, the trustee can make distributions without fear of an unknown creditor's claim.

The bottom line: trust distributions must be made within a reasonable timeframe, but the term "reasonable" is not defined. Each case will be different depending on the type of assets owned by the trust and the type of debts and expenses of the trust.

DISTRIBUTEE LIABILITY

A quick note on distributee liability: for those situations where a trustee fears some future claim by an unknown creditor, it may be helpful to point out Probate Code sections 19400 to 19403—distributee liability. These sections provide that if a creditor comes forward at a later date (and if the trustee did NOT use the creditor claims procedure described in the previous section), then any liability on the creditor's claim flows through to the beneficiaries. In other words, the beneficiaries will be liable to pay a creditor to the extent the beneficiaries received distributions from the trust.

To be clear, this does NOT mean that you, as a beneficiary, are liable for the debts of the trust. It just means that if a creditor is discovered, and the trust has distributed all the assets to you, then you have to use those distributed assets to pay the trust creditor. The debt follows the assets that were distributed. Once you pay everything you received from the trust to a creditor, then you are not obligated to pay anything else. It is only the distributed assets that the creditor can obtain, not your own personal money or assets.

The next time a trustee tells you a distribution cannot be made because some unknown creditor may arise in the future, point them to distributee liability. "Not to worry," you can say, "because the debt will be paid by me, the beneficiary, from the distributed assets, if that should occur." Another trustee excuse deflated, thanks to the California probate code.

Death and Taxes

Two further issues can delay a trust distribution: death and taxes.

Death of a beneficiary: by death, I am referring to the death of a beneficiary after the settlor has died. Naturally, none of the trust assets are distributed (usually) while the settlor is living. But once the settlor dies, then distributions must take place within a reasonable time.

When a beneficiary dies, there can be a further delay for a number of reasons. The first question is whether the beneficiary's estate is entitled to the deceased beneficiary's distribution. Typically, a beneficiary's estate will receive the beneficiary's distribution if the beneficiary survived the settlor. But that can vary based on the trust terms.

For example, if the trust requires a beneficiary to survive a settlor for a certain amount of time, then that must occur. Some trusts will state that a beneficiary must survive the settlor for sixty days (or ninety days or 120 days). If the beneficiary dies before sixty days of the settlor's death, then the beneficiary's gift is extinguished.

Some trusts will require a beneficiary to survive until the assets are distributed (this is very rare, but I have seen it). In that case, a beneficiary's death prior to distribution of trust assets will extinguish the beneficiary's gift.

If the beneficiary's estate is still entitled to a distribution after death, then the next question is—where does the distribution go? For example, should the distribution be paid to the beneficiary's executor or trustee, the beneficiary's wife, or directly to the beneficiary's children? That all depends on how the beneficiary set up their estate plan (trust, will, or whatever they have).

The wonderful world of taxes: There are numerous types of taxes you have to consider: estate tax, income tax, and real property tax, just to name a few. As of 2018, federal estate tax only applies to estates valued in excess of $11.2 million for a single person or $22.4 million for married couples. Most estates do not exceed these amounts; therefore, no federal estate tax is due.

Some states have an inheritance tax, but not California. Therefore, once you pay any federal estate tax, there will be no further estate or inheritance tax due to the State of California.

Income tax applies to any income received by the trust or estate. Bear in mind that anything you receive as an inheritance is NOT subject to income tax. But any income received by the trust estate (such as investment income, bank interest, dividends, gain on real estate sales) is subject to income tax. That income must be reported by the trust using IRS form 1041 (and California Form 541). Any income tax is then paid either by the trust or passed through to the beneficiary(ies) to pay. The tax payment depends on the type of trust and the amount of distributions made to trust beneficiaries during the tax year.

Property tax can be an issue for beneficiaries who are given a gift of real estate. If you intend to keep the real estate, then there may be a significant increase in property taxes. There are ways to avoid an increase in property taxes, such as filing a parent-to-child exclusion for the transfer of real estate. But there are deadlines by which this type of exclusion must be requested from the tax assessor's office. Be sure to request any property tax exclusions promptly.

All of these tax issues must be addressed and properly reported (plus any taxes paid) before final distributions can take place. But some money/assets can be distributed before taxes are finalized. It all depends on the amount of tax liability expected and from whom the tax payments will be required.

TRUSTEE REMOVAL AND SUSPENSION

If you fail to receive a trust distribution, you may want to consider filing a petition to remove the trustee. A trust beneficiary has the right to file a petition with the court seeking to remove the trustee. A beneficiary can also ask the court to suspend the trustee pending removal. Removal usually requires a trial to be conducted so the court can hear evidence. Since it can take anywhere from eight months to a couple of years to have a trial, suspension may be necessary to safeguard the trust until the removal trial is finalized.

Removing a trustee is not so easy. For starters, the trustee is presumed to be the settlor's chosen person, so the burden rests with the beneficiary to prove why the trustee cannot act. Under Probate Code section 15642(b), a trustee may be removed from office where:

1. The trustee has committed a breach of the trust;

2. The trustee is insolvent or otherwise unfit to administer the trust;

3. Hostility or lack of cooperation among co-trustees impairs the administration of the trust;

4. The trustee fails or declines to act;

5. The trustee's compensation is excessive under the circumstances;

6. The sole trustee is a prohibited beneficiary (for example, the person who drafted the trust cannot act as sole trustee);

7. The trustee is substantially unable to manage the trust's financial resources or is otherwise substantially unable to execute properly the duties of the office;

8. The trustee is substantially unable to resist fraud or undue influence; or

9. For other good cause.

While this list of removal grounds seems ominous, it is up to the beneficiary to prove the existence of one of them before removal will occur. Further, the court has discretion to excuse whatever breach occurred and allow the trustee to continue acting if the court chooses to do so. That means the beneficiary must not only prove the existence of a ground for removal, but it also helps for them to establish that future harm will result to the trust if the trustee is not removed.

Under Probate Code section 15642(e) the court can suspend the trustee and appoint either a receiver or temporary trustee to act until trial on the removal issue occurs.

The most likely grounds for removal of a trustee is theft. Anytime you can show with financial evidence that the trustee has misappropriated trust funds, you are far more likely to obtain both suspension and removal of the trustee.

Failure to distribute can also lead to suspension and removal, provided that, the distribution is substantially overdue.

But removal is not your only option. A beneficiary also has the right to seek instructions from the court.

PETITION FOR INSTRUCTIONS

Under Probate Code section 17200, a trust beneficiary has the right to petition the probate court regarding the "internal affairs of the trust." In other words, you can ask the court to order the trustee to do (or not do) something. Lawyers generally refer to this as a "petition for instructions."

Using a petition for instructions, you can ask the court to order the trustee to do anything the trust requires. For example, if you are owed a $500,000 trust distribution but the trustee refuses, you can ask the court to order the trustee to distribute. If the trustee has a reason to withhold distribution, they can make that argument to the court. But the court will ultimately decide what amount will be distributed. Once you have the court order, then the trustee must comply, and you no longer have to argue over the distribution.

The same goes for things like providing copies of trust documents, financial information, accountings, investment decisions, and the creation and funding of sub-trusts. Anytime the trust (or the Probate Code) requires an action, and the trustee fails to do so, the court can step in and order that action to take place. But the court will not do so on its own. It is up to you, the beneficiary, to bring a petition for instructions seeking a court order.

The benefit of a petition for instructions is that you don't have to prove a breach of trust exists. Whether the trustee breached a duty or not, the requested action can be ordered. And at the end of the day, that is what you want—a distribution to occur. This is a much easier petition to prove and it can achieve your result a bit more quickly, at times, than a lawsuit to remove a trustee, or suing for breach of trust.

In the end, trust assets must be distributed to the trust beneficiaries. Especially in the case of Tom and Brian, where the trust required an outright distribution of assets. In trust law, outright means to give the money, real estate, stocks, bonds, jewelry, whatever else is in the trust to the beneficiaries. Tom's act of holding onto the trust property, and thinking he can hold onto it indefinitely, is just wrong. But notice: no one is going to make Tom comply with the terms of the trust, except Brian. Brian can combat trustee abuse here by taking action in court.

Unfortunately, it is Brian's burden to bring this abuse to light. Yes, Tom should comply with his legal obligations and distribute trust assets out to Brian without Brian having to force the issue in court. The whole purpose of trusts is to allow a smooth transfer of assets after death without court supervision. And yet, Tom, like many bad trustees, refuses to obey the law and chooses instead to ignore Brian. That's where our court system comes into play. Tom can ignore Brian, but Tom cannot ignore a judge once the matter is filed in court. It takes effort to stand up and fight against a bad trustee, but it can be done, and done successfully.

Along with distribution of trust assets, a trustee also has a duty to account to the beneficiaries. The next topic of beneficiary abuse: a trustee's duty to provide trust financial information and a trust accounting to the beneficiaries.

Chapter 2

Abuse Involving the Provision of Accountings to Beneficiaries

In this chapter we will discuss a trustee's failure to account and provide information to trust beneficiaries. We start with a basic understanding of the trust law we will apply to this problem.

THE BASICS OF CALIFORNIA TRUST ACCOUNTINGS

The trustee of a California trust has a duty to keep beneficiaries reasonably informed of the trust and its administration. The trustee must also account to all current income or principal beneficiaries (1) at least annually, (2) upon termination of a trust, or (3) upon a change in trustee.

A trust, by its terms, can waive the right to an accounting, but a court can still order an accounting to be created where a beneficiary shows that a breach of trust is likely to have occurred.

Trust Accountings Hypothetical: Neil and Leonard as Abused Beneficiaries

Let's consider a hypothetical situation to demonstrate the problems that arise and the options you have when confronted with a California trustee who fails to account. After the hypothetical, we will discuss trust accountings in more detail.

For the last eight years, Burt has been the trustee of a trust created to benefit Neil and Leonard, two brothers. The trust terms do not mention anything about providing trust accountings to the beneficiaries. The trust terms also require the trust to continue for ten years and then distribute the assets outright to Neil and Leonard equally. The trust has two more years to go before distribution is required.

The trust assets originally consisted of a six-unit apartment building and an investment portfolio with conservative investments. Eight years ago when Burt began acting as trustee, the apartment building was valued at $2 million and the investment portfolio was worth $500,000.

Neil and Leonard have never received an accounting from Burt and do not have any recent financial information. Neil thinks that the apartment building had a small mortgage against it of $50,000 when Burt took over as trustee.

At first, Neil and Leonard were each receiving $3,000 per month from the trust. But two years ago that stopped. The distributions dropped to $1,000 per month for a while and then stopped altogether. Neil and Leonard asked for more trust distributions, but they never received a straight answer from Burt on why the distributions had stopped.

In response, Neil and Leonard demanded a trust accounting. First, Burt claimed that an accounting was not required of him because the trust was silent as to accountings. Then Burt said he would provide them with an accounting.

Last month Burt sent Neil and Leonard a one-page spreadsheet that Burt claims is the trust "accounting." The spreadsheet has the apartment building on it with an estimated value of $2 million, but it also lists a mortgage against the apartment building for $1.5 million. All the rent from the apartment building is being used to pay the mortgage payments, which explains why the distributions have stopped.

The spreadsheet also lists $50,000 in cash, and five separate so-called investments, each with a listed value of $400,000. On paper, the trust appears to have a gross value of $4,050,000.

Neil and Leonard are surprised to see the mortgage on the apartment building because they were never told about it. They are also surprised to see the five investments, so they ask the trustee to provide more explanation on the investments. Burt tells them that the investments are "private placements," which allow individuals with a high net worth to invest in securities that are not regulated by the government. Unfortunately, Burt believes that all five of the investments have failed and may not be recouped by the trust. On the other hand, some of the investments may pay off if the trust retains them for twenty years or more.

Neil and Leonard are alarmed at this news. The trust is supposed to distribute all assets to them outright in two years. They also wonder if they have been given all the information about the trust finances. Even though they do not know what a proper trust accounting looks like, the one-page spreadsheet does not look correct to them.

NEIL AND LEONARD'S OPTIONS

It appears that Burt has taken a substantial loan against the apartment building to invest in highly risky investments. And the original $500,000 investment portfolio seems to be gone. What can Neil and Leonard do to find out the full extent of the trust's financial dealings? Here are the options:

1. **Petition for accounting.** Petition the court to order Burt to prepare and file a formal trust accounting;

2. **Petition for information.** Petition the court to order Burt to provide all financial statements for the last eight years;

3. **Subpoena information.** Subpoena all bank and financial records from the financial institutions for the trust for the past eight years;

4. **Trustee removal.** Petition to remove Burt as trustee; or

5. **Petition for damages.** Petition to seek damages against Burt for breach of trust.

OUR RECOMMENDATIONS ON ENFORCING TRUST ACCOUNTINGS

Options 1 and 2: our firm would recommend that Neil and Leonard start with options 1 (accounting) and 2 (information). A proper trust accounting is desperately needed in this case because Neil and Leonard have no idea what has occurred in their trust assets. It seems that their $500,000 investment portfolio is gone. And the $1.5 million in loans against the apartment buildings appear to have been invested in risky private placements that are now worthless. The best way to begin to understand what has occurred is with a proper trust accounting.

Option 3: subpoenaing financial information is also important, but you cannot issue a subpoena until you first file a lawsuit in court. Once you file a petition demanding a proper trust accounting, then you have the power to issue subpoenas. You would want to issue subpoenas to every bank, financial institution, and investment institution you can. This process will allow you to obtain information from the source so you can begin to figure out what happened in this trust administration.

Option 4: trustee removal could be brought at the beginning of the case, but removal is not easy to obtain. It is much easier to obtain trustee removal after you uncover the financial problems and mistakes. As such, we recommend forcing an accounting and subpoenaing financial information before filing to remove the trustee in most cases. But that is not always the case, so evaluate your removal options and include that in your petition if you think it necessary to do so upfront.

Option 5: the final option, petition for damages, will come later. Again, once you have an accounting, then you can file objections to the accounting asking the court to surcharge the trustee. You can also file a separate petition for breach of trust after you uncover the financial information that supports your claims. You could bring a petition for damages upfront, but that depends on your particular case. In Neil and Leonard's case, we would wait until more financial information comes to light before filing a petition for damages.

THE LAW OF TRUST ACCOUNTINGS

The right to a trust accounting in California is provided under the terms of the Probate Code and under the terms of the trust document (subject to any overriding provisions of the Probate Code).

For starters, California Probate Code section 16060 provides that the trustee has a duty to keep the beneficiaries of the trust reasonably informed of the trust and its administration.

Right to information: further, under California Probate Code section 16061, except as provided in Section 16069, on reasonable request by a beneficiary, the trustee must provide information to the trust beneficiary relating to the administration of the trust relevant to the beneficiary's interest. This means that a beneficiary has the right to all information, including financial information, relating to the beneficiary's share of the trust.

The right to information under section 16061 is separate from the right to an accounting, but the two requirements complement each other. An accounting, discussed below, is a formal report of information given in a format specified by the California Probate Code. Whereas the right to information under section 16061 goes beyond the mere accounting requirements and includes things like copies of bank statements, escrow closing statements, property management statements—any documents the trustee has that are relevant to the beneficiary's share. The right to information also includes information such as a description from the trustee of actions they have taken.

Many people overlook the right to information and focus solely on the right to accounting. At times, the underlying information is more valuable, and more helpful, than a formal accounting. Of course, it never hurts to ask for both, but don't underestimate the right to information—it can be a powerful tool to uncover trustee misdeeds.

Right to formal accounting: generally speaking, a trustee is required to provide a trust accounting at least annually. Accountings are also required at the termination of a trust and upon a change of trustee. (See California Probate Code section 16062(a).)

The trustee is not required to account, however, to the beneficiary of a revocable trust for the period of time that the trust remains revocable, or where the trustee and the beneficiary are the same person.

The trustee is also not required to account where the trust document has a specific provision that waives the accounting requirement (California Probate Code section 16062). This is a fairly common provision in many trusts. It is unfortunate because beneficiaries should always be given the right to an accounting if the trust settlor wants to ensure their trustee is being kept accountable.

Luckily, even where a trust document waives the accounting requirement, the court can still order the trustee to account where the beneficiary is able to show a reasonable likelihood that a material breach of trust has occurred.

Finally, the trustee is not required to account where a beneficiary has waived the right to an accounting in writing. However, the beneficiary has the right to withdraw the waiver, in which case all transactions that take place after the withdrawal has been made are subject to accounting. Further, the court can compel an accounting where a waiver of account has been made with a showing that it is reasonably likely that a material breach of trust has occurred.

The bottom line: trust accounting requirements are quite liberal in order to protect the rights of the beneficiaries. And a formal accounting is usually the best way to learn what damages, if any, have been incurred by the trust.

How to Demand a Formal Accounting

The trustee is supposed to provide you, the beneficiary, with trust accountings when they are due—for example, at the end of each year in which the trustee has acted. But where a trustee fails or refuses to account, then you have to take action.

To demand an accounting, either you, or your lawyer (if you have hired a lawyer), must do so in writing. Don't worry, there are no special words you have to use. You can start this process yourself even if you have not hired a lawyer yet (see chapter 7 for an example of a letter demanding an accounting). All you need to do is tell the trustee, "I want an accounting," and that suffices. Of course, you can say more than that, but the point being—there is no magic language.

Once you demand the accounting in writing, the trustee has sixty days in which to provide an accounting (California Probate Code section 17200(b)(6)(C)). If the trustee fails to do so, then you have the right to file a petition with the probate court under Probate Code section 17200 and ask the court to order the trustee to account. And that's how you obtain an accounting.

ACCOUNTING FORMAT

A trust accounting is unique, meaning Burt's single-page spreadsheet that he supplied to Neil and Leonard doesn't suffice. The formal requirements for a trust accounting can be found at Probate Code sections 16063 and 1061 (all accountings to be filed in court must comply with section 1061).

Under Probate Code section 16063(a), all accountings must contain the following information regardless of whether they will be filed with the court:

1. A statement of receipts and disbursements of principal and income that have occurred during the last complete fiscal year of the trust or since the last accounting.

2. A statement of the assets and liabilities of the trust as of the end of the last complete fiscal year of the trust or as of the end of the period covered by the accounting.

3. The trustee's compensation for the last complete fiscal year of the trust or since the last accounting.

4. The agents hired by the trustee, their relationship to the trustee, if any, and their compensation, for the last complete fiscal year of the trust or since the last accounting.

5. A statement that the recipient of the accounting may petition the court pursuant to section 17200 to obtain a court review of the accounting and of the acts of the trustee.

6. A statement that claims against the trustee for breach of trust may not be made after the expiration of three years from the date the beneficiary receives an accounting or report disclosing facts giving rise to the claim.

For court-approved accountings, the specific requirements of Probate Code section 1061 must also be followed (see chapter 7 for a sample of a proper trust accounting that meets the requirements of section 1061). Section 1061 provides a format that starts with all charges, meaning trust assets that came into the trustee's possession (the items the trustee is charged with managing). Charges include (1) trust assets (money, stocks, bonds, real estate, jewelry, etc.) held by the trustee at the start of the accounting period, (2) receipts received by the trustee during the accounting period, (3) gains on sale of assets that occurred during the accounting period, and (4) any other trust property obtained by the trustee.

Next all credits are listed. Credits are items that the trustee is credited with in managing the trust assets. The credit side includes (1) disbursements (which is the same as bills paid), (2) distributions (payments to the trust beneficiaries), (3) losses on the sale of any capital assets, and (4) trust assets held by the trustee at the end of the accounting period.

The total amount of charges must be the same as the total amount of credits—this is how you know the accounting balances. If the two numbers do not match, then the accounting does not balance.

Each of the items of charges and credits must have its own schedule that provides details. For example, if the trustee reports that they disbursed $100,000 on bills during the accounting period, then you would want to know what bills they paid. There should be a schedule of disbursements that provides the date each bill was paid, to whom it was paid, what it was for, and the amount paid. You should be able to review the disbursement schedule and determine how the trust money was spent.

The same is true for receipts, distributions, gains and losses, and property on hand. Each category must have its own detail schedule, so you know exactly how the numbers reported on the accounting were obtained.

Beware that not every certified public accountant (CPA) knows how to create a proper trust accounting. Many CPAs know the proper format, but some do not, so inquire beforehand to determine if your CPA knows what to do. Keep in mind that trust accountings are unique— they are unlike corporate accountings. If you request a trust accounting and you receive a balance sheet and profit and loss statement, then you have the wrong documents. Balance sheets and profit and loss statements are not used for trust accountings. Instead, it must follow the requirements of the Probate Code under sections 16063 and 1061.

FORMAL OR INFORMAL ACCOUNTING

In the world of trusts and wills, we trust lawyers often talk about formal vs. informal accountings. Typically, when trust lawyers refer to a "formal" accounting, we mean an accounting filed in probate court subject to court approval. Whereas an "informal" accounting is pretty much the same document that is not filed in court.

More broadly, however, an "informal" trust accounting could be just about anything. Burt's one-page summary to Neil and Leonard could suffice as an informal trust accounting, if Neil and Leonard accepted it and didn't need any further information. The problem for Neil and Leonard, however, is that Burt's one-page summary did not fully describe all the financial transactions that had taken place. The best accountings are always those that follow the format and information rules under the Probate Code. Even where an accounting is not being filed for court approval, the format of an accounting is important if you are going to rely on it to settle a trust.

The reason many people avoid formal trust accountings—meaning those filed for court approval—is the cost of doing so. It takes time and money to draft a petition asking the court to approve a formal trust accounting. But where you have discrepancies or breaches of trust, you may need the court's help to surcharge the trustee and force them to repay for any damages incurred to the trust. Since the formal accounting requires court approval, the court has the power to surcharge the trustee as part of its process to approve the accounting.

Of course, you can also file a petition for breach of trust using the information you have from an informal accounting. But the court may require the accounting to be filed in court for court review. So a court-approved accounting is often the better way to go when you suspect the trustee has caused damage to your trust.

Where, however, there are no damage claims against the trustee, then an informal accounting may be sufficient to ensure the trust finances are sound and then close the trust administration. It all depends on the facts and circumstances surrounding your trust estate.

TIMEFRAMES FOR OBJECTING

Once you receive an accounting, or any written report of trust activity, you only have three years in which to object to all transactions reported in the accounting and seek damages against the trustee. If you wait longer than three years, then you are forever barred from suing the trustee for damages.

This statute of limitations for holding trustee's liable for breach of trust is an important deadline. Anytime you receive any trust information in writing from the trustee—regardless of whether it is a written trust accounting—you must think of this three-year deadline and consider whether you need to take action in court to preserve your rights.

Furthermore, some trustees have the power to shorten the statute of limitations period from three years to six months. California Probate Code section 16461 allows trust settlors to add this exception to any trust the settlor creates, but this specific exception must be stated in the trust document. If the trust document does not allow the trustee to shorten the objection period, then it does not apply.

Some settlors add the section 16461 exception to their trust because they want to protect the trustee from "unreasonable" beneficiaries by allowing the trustee to shorten the objection time period to six months. Unfortunately, this exception can backfire when a bad trustee is managing the trust estate. To further compound the problem, most settlors have no idea this provision is included in their trust, or what the potential negative consequences can be from such a provision. Most trusts are attorney-drafted, and there are many attorneys who believe it is helpful to protect the trustee from future lawsuits. But protecting all trustees comes at a cost of protecting some abusive trustees.

Next, the trustee must also include a warning about the shortened period in the accounting that is provided to the beneficiaries. If both of these requirements are met, then the trust beneficiaries only have six months in which to file a lawsuit seeking damages against their trustee for any actions reported in the trust accounting.

In summary, don't sit on your rights. If you receive a trust accounting, be sure to review it carefully and decide quickly if court action is necessary to protect your rights. Like Neil and Leonard, there is only one way to force a trustee like Burt to answer for their bad acts: file a petition in court. Once the lawsuit is filed, Neil and Leonard's lawyer then has the power to issue subpoenas and obtain financial information directly from the source—banks, brokerage firms, escrow companies, etc. These source documents can tell the true tale of Burt's bad acts.

If you are in Neil and Leonard's shoes and don't know what actions to take next, feel free to contact us at Albertson & Davidson, LLP. We have plenty of resources to help you stand up and fight back for your rightful inheritance. You don't need to be the victim of a bad trustee, you have legal rights, but it is up to you to enforce those legal rights.

Providing an accounting to the beneficiaries is not the only duty of a trustee. Also, a trustee must follow the trust terms. The next topic of beneficiary abuse: a trustee's duty to follow the terms of the trust.

Chapter 3

Abuse Involving the Following of Trust Terms

This chapter addresses a trustee's failure to follow the trust terms, especially when they are required to create sub-trusts after the death of a settlor. Let's start with a basic understanding of the trust law we will apply to this problem.

THE BASICS OF FOLLOWING CALIFORNIA TRUST TERMS

Under Probate Code section 16000, every trustee must administer the trust according to the trust instrument. That means the trustee must take all actions required of them by the trust document and by trust law.

FOLLOWING TRUST TERMS HYPOTHETICAL: DANIELLE AND JAIME AS ABUSED BENEFICIARIES

Let's consider a hypothetical situation to demonstrate the problems that arise and the options you have when confronted with a California trustee who fails to follow the trust terms. After the hypothetical, we will discuss trust terms in more detail.

In 2001, Rene and Phil created a joint trust. At the time, their estate was worth $3 million, and they were worried about the surviving spouse having to pay federal estate tax upon the other spouse's death. As a result, the joint trust Rene and Phil created had a provision that required the creation and funding of two sub-trusts after the first spouse died.

Under the trust, once the first of Rene and Phil passes away, the trust assets are divided into two equal shares. One share is to be funded into a survivor's trust, which remains a revocable trust and is held for the benefit of the surviving spouse. The other share is to be funded into a bypass trust, which is an irrevocable trust. The bypass trust is held to benefit the surviving spouse during their lifetime, and then the remaining assets pass to the children equally. Rene has no children, but Phil has two children from a prior marriage, Danielle and Jaime. Under the trust terms Jaime's share is held in a separate trust for his benefit.

In 2015, Phil dies, and Rene takes over as the sole successor trustee of their joint trust. Unfortunately, Rene does not seek the advice of an attorney, and she is not aware that the survivor's trust and the bypass trust have to be created after Phil's death. Instead, Rene keeps administering the trust assets for her own benefit as if nothing has changed.

Over the next year, Danielle and Jaime begin to wonder what has become of their father's share of the estate, so they make multiple inquires with Rene about it. Rene takes offense to these inquires and tells both kids to mind their own business. Rene refuses to provide copies of the trust to the children and stops returning their calls.

In February 2016, Rene decides to leave the entire estate to her two sisters, Betty and Linda, instead of the children. Rene meets a lawyer who drafts a simple trust amendment changing the beneficiaries of the trust from the children to Betty and Linda. The lawyer does not discuss the survivor's trust or bypass trust with Rene because he did not carefully review Phil and Rene's trust, so he did not notice the sub-trust requirements. The lawyer simply prepares the trust amendment.

In August 2016, Rene dies and Betty takes over as successor trustee of the trust. Betty reads the trust amendment and believes that she and her sister, Linda, are the sole beneficiaries. When Danielle and Jaime ask for a copy of the trust document, Betty provides them with a copy of the trust and the trust amendment.

Danielle and Jaime consult a lawyer. The lawyer notices that Rene was supposed to create a bypass trust after Phil's death, but she failed to do so. Since the bypass trust was supposed to be irrevocable, Rene had no power to amend that part of the trust. The lawyer believes that Danielle and Jaime have a claim to force Betty to hand over at least one-half of the trust estate in spite of the trust amendment Rene created.

THE OPTIONS

It now appears that Rene has ignored her duties as trustee and failed to create and fund the bypass trust. What can Danielle and Jaime do to obtain their fair share of the trust estate? Here are the options:

1. **Contest amendment.** File a trust contest petition challenging the validity of the trust amendment.

2. **Petition for instructions.** File a petition for instructions to enforce the terms of the bypass trust.

3. **Financial elder abuse lawsuit.** File for financial elder abuse against Betty (Rene's sister).

4. **Creditor's claim.** File a creditor's claim with Rene's estate for one-half the value of the trust.

5. **Letter writing.** Hire a lawyer to write a letter to Betty asking that she distribute one-half of the trust estate to Danielle and Jaime.

OUR EXPERT RECOMMENDATION

Here, Rene failed to follow the trust terms. The trust required that one-half of the estate be transferred into the bypass trust after Phil died. The bypass trust would have supported Rene during her lifetime, but Rene couldn't amend the bypass trust to disinherit Jaime and Danielle. That means the trust amendment Rene signed could only affect the survivor's trust, not the bypass trust.

Option 2: the first action we would recommend Danielle and Jaime take is to file a petition for instructions. A petition for instructions is simply a request that the court take a certain action. Here, the action would be to force Betty to create and fund assets into the bypass trust as required by the trust terms. Or it could be setting aside assets equal to the amount that should have been placed in the bypass trust and distributing those assets to Jaime and Danielle. As a judge once told us, it is never too late to do the right thing. So long as there are assets still in the trust, the court can order the trustee to follow the trust terms and, thereby, give Jaime and Danielle the assets that should have been held in the bypass trust.

Option 1: filing to contest the amendment should not be necessary if you follow option 2 instead. Option 1 is problematic for Jaime and Danielle because it could trigger the trust's no-contest clause. Let's discuss the no-contest clause a bit further.

Rene created a trust amendment that purports to change the entire distribution of the trust to Betty and Linda. That amendment was not possible as to half of the trust estate because half of the estate was supposed to be transferred into the irrevocable bypass trust. The bypass trust could not be revoked or amended by Rene. However, that does not mean the trust amendment is an invalid document. The amendment could still be valid and apply to the portion of the trust that remained revocable—the survivor's trust.

If Jaime and Danielle challenge the validity of the trust amendment in court, they would have to base that challenge on a legal claim, such as lack of capacity and/or undue influence. Under Probate Code section 21310, if you challenge the validity of a trust or trust amendment based on lack of capacity or undue influence, then you may be disinherited under the trust's no-contest clause.

If Jaime and Danielle challenge the trust amendment and win, then they would likely receive the entire trust estate. If Jaime and Danielle challenge the trust amendment and lose, they would likely lose everything—even their share of the bypass trust.

Jaime and Danielle can protect themselves by simply not challenging the validity of the trust amendment. For these reasons, we would probably go with option 2, petition for instructions, rather than option 1. This would allow Jaime and Danielle to receive their share of the bypass trust without risking disinheritance by challenging the trust amendment directly.

Option 3: a financial elder abuse lawsuit can be brought against a party who obtains a gift under a trust by exercising undue influence against the trust settlor—in this case Rene. Such a lawsuit made against Betty would not work because Betty did not participate in the creation of the trust amendment. It seems that Betty came in after the amendment was complete and started to administer the trust as successor trustee. There are no facts to support that Betty exercised undue influence against Rene to create the trust amendment.

Option 5: a letter writing campaign rarely works. Many people think that if a lawyer writes a letter to Betty, she will do the right thing and return half of the estate to Jamie and Danielle. In our experience that occurs about 10% of the time. More often, the letter is just ignored and nothing happens. Filing in court is the only way to seek a court order and force Betty to comply with the correct terms of the trust.

Option 4: filing a creditor's claim typically is done with trusts when one party claims to be owed money by a person who has died. For the two children, this is an interesting option if the trust assets had been transferred out of the trust before Rene's death (I'll explain this point shortly). Rene, as trustee, had the duty while she was alive to properly administer the trust and follow the trust terms. When Rene failed to follow the trust terms, she breached her duties as trustee. If Rene were still alive, Jaime and Danielle could sue Rene for breach of duty. After death, however, the only way to file suit is by filing a creditor's claim in Rene's probate estate—meaning a separate legal case filed in probate court in addition to the trust case.

The problem with a creditor's claim is that it could trigger the trust's no-contest clause. Under Probate Code section 21311(a)(3), the filing of a creditor's claim, or the prosecution of an action based on it, could trigger a no-contest clause. The trust must have a no-contest clause that specifically includes this provision for this to apply. But assuming Rene and Phil's trust has this provision, then the creditor's claim could disinherit Jaime and Danielle.

A creditor's claim may be the only route to take if the assets were moved out of the trust prior to Rene's death. For example, if Rene created an entirely new trust and transferred all her assets to this new trust (rather than doing a trust amendment), then a petition for instructions (option 2) would not work. Remember that the petition for instructions was going to force Betty to follow the trust terms, but if the assets are in a new trust that does not have the same terms as the old trust, then a petition for instructions is not helpful.

Worse yet, if Rene emptied the trust and put the assets into her individual name, then the petition for instructions has no usefulness because there are no assets in the original trust. Forcing the trustee of a trust to distribute assets to Jaime and Danielle only works if the trust has assets to distribute. No assets in a trust equals no assets to Jaime and Danielle.

If there are no assets left in the original trust created by Phil and Rene, then a creditor's claim would be required—indeed, it would be the only viable option to enforce the trust terms. The claim would be made against Rene's estate for breach of trust, and the damages would equal one-half of the trust assets. Once that claim is asserted in Rene's estate, and if it is granted by the court, then Jaime and Danielle can enforce that claim against all assets in the probate estate and all assets transferred to any other trust created by Rene during her lifetime.

As you can see, the option Jaime and Danielle pursue is dependent not just on the trust terms they want to enforce, but also on the location of assets at the time of Rene's death. Assets still held in the original trust created by Phil and Rene are much easier to attack and gain distribution from than assets that were transferred out of the original trust. There are ways to force a distribution, but the beneficiaries must choose options based on how the assets are titled at the time of Rene's death.

THE LAW OF FOLLOWING TRUST TERMS

Probate Code section 16000 sets out the standard every trustee must follow in administering a trust estate—namely, follow the trust terms. Seems like an easy mandate, and yet many private trustees violate this simple directive.

Many people do not understand that trusts typically require different actions at different times throughout the life cycle of the trust. There are provisions that apply while the trust settlor(s) is still living, provisions that apply after a settlor dies, and even provisions that apply long after the settlor is gone, such as sub-trusts created for children and grandchildren.

You can think of the initial trust estate created by the settlor as the main trust. This is the part of the trust that controls the assets of the trust estate for the benefit of the settlor(s). When a settlor dies, there is a period of administration (sometimes referred to as the administrative trust—it is the same trust as before, just in an administrative phase). During trust administration, the trustee is supposed to take all actions required by the trust document, including creating sub-trusts.

Commonly created sub-trusts include survivor's trusts (for the surviving spouse), bypass trusts (to hold the assets of the deceased spouse), marital trusts (also to hold assets of the deceased spouse), disclaimer trusts (to hold any property a beneficiary decides to disclaim or turn down), children's trusts (held for the benefit of kids), and grandchildren's trust (held for the benefit of grandchildren). Each of these sub-trusts has a different set of rules and a different set of beneficiaries.

Each sub-trust must be created by opening new financial accounts in the name of the sub-trust and transferring assets into those accounts. Or in the case of real estate, the deed is transferred into the name of the appropriate sub-trust. Each trust will require its own tax identification number from the IRS for tax-reporting purposes.

Creating sub-trusts is not hard to do, but it does take deliberate action—the sub-trusts don't create themselves. And if a trust mandates the creation of sub-trusts, then it is the trustee's duty to follow the trust terms and create the sub-trusts. Failure to do so is a breach of trust by the trustee.

CREATION OF SUB-TRUSTS—
MANDATORY VS. DISCRETIONARY

Typically, when a trust provides for the creation of sub-trusts, it is a mandatory requirement. You will know if it is mandatory by use of the word "shall," as opposed to using the word "may." If a trust says a trustee shall create a sub-trust, then it must be done. If a trust says a trustee may create a sub-trust, then it is up to the trustee's discretion to do so.

In the case of survivor's trusts, bypass trusts, and marital trusts, their creation is almost always mandatory. Once the first spouse of a married couple dies, the sub-trusts must be created to protect the surviving spouse from the imposition of estate taxes and to ensure that assets pass to the deceased spouse's children.

There are some sub-trusts, however, that are discretionary. For example, disclaimer trusts are created when a surviving spouse decides they do not want to take possession of assets. Usually this is done for estate tax purposes, but it could also be done to give assets to the deceased spouse's children. In any event, once a spouse disclaims an asset, then the disclaimer trust is created, and it acts pretty much the same as a bypass trust.

There are also various generation-skipping transfer trusts that can be created at the discretion of the trustee if it would be advantageous to do so from a tax perspective.

Finally, there are times when the trust will state that no physical separation of assets is necessary in creating sub-trusts. This may occur when the entire trust estate is going to be held in a sub-trust for a child. Even though the trust is technically a child's trust, the trust document may state that a trustee need not retitle all the assets if it would be inconvenient to do so. But even though the assets are not retitled in the name of the child's trust, the trust estate is still held and administered under the trust terms for the benefit of the child.

Obviously, where several sub-trusts are required to be created, then physical segregation of the assets is a must. In that case, each sub-trust should receive its share of assets retitled in the name of each respective sub-trust.

HOW DO YOU KNOW IF THE TERMS ARE BEING FOLLOWED?

The only way to ensure the trust document is being properly adminis-tered is to ask for confirmation. First, you need a copy of the trust document, so you know what actions are supposed to take place. Second, you need copies of all financial accounts and deeds to ensure that each sub-trust has a newly created account funded with the appro-priate amount of assets. Third, you need a trust accounting. The trustee must be able to account for how the assets were valued and how they were distributed to the various sub-trusts.

If you do not have the trust documents and the financial information confirming proper sub-trust creation, then you do not know if the trustee has acted properly. It is critically important for you to obtain confirming information. Until you have confirmation, you have no idea what has occurred. And it is much easier to fix a problem earlier rather than later. Take the time and put in the effort to obtain the financial information you need to confirm the trustee has acted appropriately.

IF A TRUSTEE REFUSES TO FOLLOW THE TRUST TERMS . . .

A. Petition for instructions. If you are a beneficiary of the trust, then you have a right to file a petition for instructions asking the court to order the trustee to comply with the trust terms. To bring a petition, you need to prepare a written brief to the court outlining your problem. You need to discuss what the trust terms require, where the trustee has failed to follow the terms, and then request a court order.

After you file your petition, you will need to mail notice of your hearing and a copy of your petition to the trustee and all other interested parties (that is, everyone named as a beneficiary of the trust). The court will give you a hearing date, usually forty-five to sixty days after you file the petition. You must appear in person at your hearing and make your argument to the court.

After your hearing, the court can order the trustee to comply with the trust terms. You can even ask the court to order the trustee to value the assets, or you can value them yourself and ask the court to use your values. Once the asset values are determined, then the sub-trusts can be funded with the appropriate assets. Again, be sure you receive confirming financial information from the trustee to ensure proper sub-trust funding has occurred.

B. *Removal and suspension.* You can also file a petition with the court seeking to remove the trustee and asking that the trustee be suspended pending removal. Since the trustee has a duty to follow the trust terms, a failure to do so subjects them to possible removal. The court has discretion on whether to remove the trustee or not, but it never hurts to ask for removal if you believe it is necessary to protect the trust estate.

DAMAGES

Can you receive damages from the trustee for their refusal to follow the trust terms? No, not really. The court can order the trustee to take all actions necessary to create and fund the sub-trusts. And the court can order that assets be placed in the proper sub-trusts. Finally, if any of the trust assets were lost or suffered damage, then the trustee can be held liable for the losses to the trust. But there are no compensatory damages (such as for pain and suffering) or punitive damages recoverable against the trustee for failing to follow the trust terms.

That may seem surprising that trustees can breach their duties, fail to follow the trust terms, and all the court can do is order them to follow the trust terms. If there is no loss or damage to the trust assets, then the trustee is not personally liable for damages. And in most cases, the trustee will not be required to pay for your attorneys' fees and costs in forcing them to take the proper actions. However, you may seek reimbursement from the trust fund, and that is often granted where your actions benefit the trust estate.

In the case of Danielle and Jaime, they have the right to force Betty to follow the trust terms. Even though Rene failed to create two sub-trusts—the survivor's trust and bypass trust—it's not too late to do the right thing. But Betty is not likely to give half the trust estate to Jaime and Danielle voluntarily. That's where the court can help resolve these issues. Jaime and Danielle can stand up and fight for their rightful share of the trust estate, provided they choose to take action in court.

In addition to following the trust terms, a California trustee is also required to follow the terms of California trust law. The next topic of beneficiary abuse: a trustee's duty to diversify trust assets as required by California trust law.

Chapter 4

Abuse Involving the Diversification of Trust Investments

Chapter 4 addresses a trustee's failure to diversify trust investments as required under California's Prudent Investor Act. As usual, let's start with a basic understanding of the trust law we will apply to this problem.

THE BASICS OF CALIFORNIA TRUST INVESTING

Under California's Prudent Investor Act, a trustee has a duty to diversify the trust investments unless it is prudent not to do so. The duty to diversify applies to all trustee investment decisions unless the trust document expressly limits or eliminates this duty.

TRUST-INVESTING HYPOTHETICAL: SAM AS ABUSED TRUSTEE

Let's consider a hypothetical situation to demonstrate the problems that arise and the options you have when confronted with a California trustee who fails to diversify trust investments. After the hypothetical, we will discuss trust diversification in more detail.

In 1994, Linda Hamilton creates a revocable living trust and transfers her ten-unit apartment building, her personal residence, and her brokerage account into the trust. Linda is named the sole trustee during her lifetime, and her CPA, Ben, is named successor trustee.

Linda has one son, Sam. Sam has physical handicaps that make it difficult to walk, but he has full mental capacity. Sam is named as the sole beneficiary of Linda's trust after Linda dies. In 2005, Linda creates a trust amendment that requires Sam's share to be held in trust for Sam's lifetime rather than distributed to him outright. Sam is named co-trustee of his trust to act with Ben. The "Sam trust" requires all income from the trust estate to be distributed to Sam, and as much of the principal as Sam needs for his health, support, maintenance, and education.

In 2010, Linda dies and Ben takes over as successor trustee of her trust. Ben reviews the trust document and 2005 trust amendment, but he decides not to create the Sam trust. Ben fails to tell Sam he is a co-trustee of the Sam trust. Instead, Ben chooses to administer the trust as if he were sole trustee.

Ben determines that the apartment building is in disrepair. Ben can either sell the apartment building and reinvest the proceeds or invest substantial money from the trust to improve the properties. Ben does not consult a financial planner; instead, he simply spends over half a million dollars repairing the apartment building. Ben also charges the trust both trustee fees and management fees to act as property manager of the apartment complex. Even after the repairs are completed, the apartment building incurs substantial expenses every month for costs of operation. The apartment generates net income of less than $50,000 per year.

After Linda's death, Sam asks Ben if he can live in Linda's home, which is part of the trust estate. Ben says no. Instead, Ben spends $100,000 of the trust money to fix up the home and then rents it for $2,500 per month, nearly $2,000 below the fair market value rent.

After the repairs to the real estate and Linda's home, the trust only has $150,000 in investments left in the brokerage account. Ben claims this money cannot be used for Sam's benefit because it must be kept in reserve to fund expenses on the apartment building.

After all the costs and fees incurred by the trust every year, Sam only receives $3,000 per month. From that money Sam must pay his rent, buy his food, and pay for a part-time caregiver. Currently the apartment building is valued at $6.5 million, and the personal residence is valued at $2 million. Ben refuses to sell any of the real estate and tells Sam he must make do with $3,000 per month because that is all the net income the trust produces.

Sam is frustrated with Ben's actions. Sam would like to have more money to provide for his health and support, but Ben refuses to sell any property. And Ben receives only $36,000 per year, which is less than 0.5% of the total trust value.

When Sam consults with a lawyer and financial planner, he is told that he is being abused. The financial planner believes the trust assets should be diversified to protect the principal and increase the amount of income available for Sam's benefit. The lawyer is shocked to learn that Sam is a named co-trustee but was never told he had the right to co-manage the trust estate.

SAM'S OPTIONS

It now appears that Ben has ignored his duty to diversify the trust assets and caused substantial harm to the trust estate. What can Sam do to recoup the losses he has sustained and to properly correct the trust investments now so no further harm comes to the trust assets? Here are the options:

1. **Petition for removal.** File a petition to remove Ben as trustee and ask the court to suspend Ben immediately pending his permanent removal.

2. **Petition for accounting.** File a petition to force Ben to prepare and file a proper trust accounting.

3. **Petition for surcharge.** File a petition to surcharge Ben for the lost profits the trust has suffered.

4. **Trust contest.** File a petition to invalidate the 2005 trust amendment.

5. **Request resignation.** Ask Ben to resign and appoint a professional trustee.

OUR EXPERT RECOMMENDATION

Sam has a big mess on his hands. On paper, Sam is a multi-millionaire and should be receiving support of more than $3,000 per month. Yet Ben has made additional distributions impossible by failing to diversify the trust assets. Currently, the trust assets are invested entirely in real estate.

Option 1: at Albertson and Davidson, LLP, we would first recommend that Sam seek Ben's removal and suspension based on Ben's failure to follow the trust terms (he never told Sam he was a co-trustee nor allowed Sam to act as co-trustee) and failure to properly diversify the trust assets. Ben has also breached the trust terms by failing to provide more substantial distributions to Sam.

For example, Sam should receive all trust income, but Sam also has a right to trust principal if he requires more money for his care and support, which these facts suggest he does. In that case, Ben has a duty to liquidate some of the real estate to make principal available for distribution. If the principal is illiquid because it is held in real estate, then Ben has a duty to sell the real estate to raise cash that can then be distributed to Sam. The same would be true if the trust owned stocks, bonds, or any other type of non-cash investment.

The problem here is that Ben is failing to treat Sam fairly. The trust was meant to benefit Sam quite generously, yet Ben has arranged the trust estate in a way that precludes Sam from accessing trust principal.

Every trustee has a duty to invest trust assets as a prudent investor would do, taking into account the purposes, terms, distributions requirements, and other circumstances of the trust (see California Probate Code section 16047(a)). Here, Ben has done none of that. Ben has invested the assets without any considerations to the distributions requirements of the trust. Ben has also blocked Sam from acting as co-trustee and having a say in how the assets are invested. The only way to remedy this problem is to remove Ben from being trustee.

Option 5: you certainly could start with option 5 and ask Ben to voluntarily resign. In our experience, that will rarely happen, but it's worth a shot. If Ben refuses, then you can proceed by filing in court for Ben's removal under option 1.

Option 2: a petition for an accounting may be desirable depending on the circumstances. The problem with requesting a full accounting in this type of case is that it could cost the trust tens of thousands of dollars to prepare the accounting. If you have access to the financial information, then preparation of a formal accounting may not be necessary.

We would also obtain financial information directly from the financial institutions by issuing subpoenas. If we can determine the financial issues based on the subpoenas, then an accounting may not be required. If there are confusing transactions or money missing, then an accounting may be required. It all depends on the circumstances of the case once you discover more information.

Option 3: a petition for surcharge may be appropriate depending on the circumstances. We would not automatically file for surcharge against Ben, but we might. It depends on (1) whether Ben stole any money from the trust, (2) whether Ben has any assets to collect from if we do file suit against him, and (3) whether there was any loss from the trust estate.

For example, Ben did invest substantial sums into the real estate, but if the real estate appreciated during the time Ben was acting as trustee, there may not be a financial loss. The real estate can now be sold, and the costs invested would be recouped in the form of financial gain. Let's assume the property increased in value from $1 million to $5 million, with $500,000 spent on improvements and upgrades to the property. The investment may be reasonable under these circumstances since the real estate achieved a gain of $4 million. As such, there may be no financial loss to the trust estate. Ben still breached his duties by refusing to sell the real estate to allow for proper diversification of investments and distributions of principal to Sam, but Ben may not have caused financial harm to the trust assets.

If, however, the real estate lost value after Ben invested $500,000 in improvements and upgrades, then Ben may be liable for that financial loss. Of course, if Ben has no money, then suing him may be a lost cause. Again, it all depends on the circumstances after you discover further information. Don't assume that you will sue the trustee for a financial loss. Instead, study the facts of your case and then make a good decision based on the likelihood of success.

Option 4: contesting the trust would never be a good option here because contesting the trust will not help with the investment problems. Also, the trust probably has a no-contest clause that would be triggered, thereby disinheriting Sam from everything if the trust terms are challenged. Sam has generous distribution terms under the trust. It is far better to enforce those distribution terms rather than contest the trust document and risk disinheritance.

THE LAW OF DIVERSIFYING TRUST ASSETS

The California Uniform Prudent Investor Act (found at Probate Code sections 16045 to 16054) imposes investment duties and rules on all California trustees. Every trustee must follow the terms of the Prudent Investor Act except to the extent excused by any express terms of the trust document.

The Uniform Prudent Investor Act requires trustees to invest trust assets as a prudent investor would by considering the purposes, terms, distribution requirements, and other circumstances of the trust. The trustee must use reasonable care, skill, and caution when investing.

The Prudent Investor Act also requires trustees to diversify the trust assets, unless under the circumstances it would be imprudent to do so. The investment rules incorporate the concept of Modern Portfolio Theory (MPT) into trust investing. Under MPT, the entire investment portfolio is considered when creating and implementing an investment plan.

In the past, each single trust investment was considered in isolation to all other trust investments. This meant that a trustee could be held liable if a single investment was viewed as imprudent. That is no longer the case under the California Uniform Prudent Investor Act. Under the act, all the investments are considered when determining whether the investment plan is prudent or not.

WHY DIVERSIFY?

Diversification is a concept widely used in MPT where the risk of loss is spread over different asset classes. To say it in plain English: don't put all your eggs in one basket. If you have all your money tied up in real estate, and real estate declines in value (as happened in 2008 during the Great Recession), then your entire investment portfolio will lose value. However, if you only have ten percent of your total investments in real estate, then a decline in real estate will only affect ten percent of your investment values. The other ninety percent can be spread out among stocks, bonds, cash, and other investment classes. By diversifying, you can manage your risk of loss by limiting the amount you invest in each type of asset.

Every trustee has a duty to distribute risk of loss by reasonable diversification of trust assets. (See Estate of Collins (1977) 72 CA 3d 663, 669.) A portfolio must be designed and implemented to take into account the proper diversification of trust assets among several asset classes.

Diversification is particularly important in trust investing where the primary goal is to maintain trust principal. Prudent trust investing still requires some income and growth potential for the investment portfolio, but protecting principal is more important for trusts because we want to protect the trust money for the beneficiaries.

For more information on diversification, take a look at this article, "Why Diversification Matters," from Fidelity: www.fidelity.com/learning-center/investment-products/mutual-funds/diversification

The Duty to Diversify—Why Is It Violated So Often?

Probate Code section 16048 requires every trustee, in making and implementing investment decisions, to diversify the investments of the trust unless under the circumstances it is prudent not to do so.

While the duty to diversify seems simple enough, it is often violated. The problems usually begin when a successor trustee takes over an existing investment portfolio. The successor trustee may believe that the investments made by the settlor (or prior trustee) must be retained or that they are automatically prudent because the settlor made the investments in the first place.

For example, assume that the settlor built and owned an apartment building for the last three decades. The settlor rented the units and lived off the rental income. And the apartment building is the only asset of the trust. After the settlor dies, the trust becomes irrevocable, and the successor trustee takes over management of the trust estate. Can the successor trustee continue to own and operate the apartment building? That depends on the circumstances.

If the trust requires the estate be held in trust for the lifetime of a child, and the child is entitled to regular income distributions, then the apartment building may not be the best investment. First, the apartment building is not diversified because it is the only asset of the trust estate. That means all the trust assets are tied up in real estate—a violation of the duty to diversify. And the only way in which to diversify the trust estate is to sell the apartment building and reinvest the proceeds.

Second, the apartment building may not provide the best return on investment. If there are substantial expenses for the apartment, then the costs may outweigh the rental income. In that event, a different investment may more easily produce income without any risk of paying expenses.

Third, the distribution requirements of the trust must be taken into account when structuring an investment portfolio. If money is needed for a beneficiary's health and support, as was true for Sam in the chapter's hypothetical, then the trustee may have to dip into principal, which can be impossible to do when the principal is real estate.

The bottom line: the successor trustee needs to make their own analysis for the proper investment approach for the trust. The trustee cannot simply maintain the status quo that the settlor created. What was good for the settlor may no longer be good for the trust beneficiary. The trust settlor had the right to violate the Prudent Investor Act because it was their money, whereas a successor trustee must follow the Prudent Investor Act because the money now belongs to the beneficiaries (especially where the trust has become irrevocable).

Once a successor trustee takes over, everything changes. The rights of the beneficiary(ies) changes, the duty to invest changes, the distribution requirements may change—it's a whole new world. If the trustee does not create and implement a proper investment plan, then the Prudent Investor Act will be violated.

THE INVESTOR POLICY STATEMENT

Nothing under the Prudent Investor Act requires a trustee to have a written investor policy statement, but every trustee should have one anyway. An investor policy statement is a written document that sets out the risk and loss tolerance of the client and the investment plan the client should use to meet their goals. Nearly every financial institution has investor policy statement forms that you can customize with the help of your financial advisor.

Under the Prudent Investor Act there are many different factors a trustee must consider when creating an investment plan. Probate Code section 16047(c) requires trustees to consider:

1. General economic conditions;

2. The possible effect of inflation and deflation;

3. The expected tax consequences of investment decisions or strategies;

4. The role that each investment or course of action plays within the overall trust portfolio;

5. The expected total return from income and the appreciation of capital;

6. Other resources of the beneficiaries known to the trustee as determined from information provided by the beneficiaries;

7. Needs for liquidity, regularity of income, and preservation or appreciation of capital; and

8. An asset's special relationship or special value, if any, to the purposes of the trust or to one or more of the beneficiaries.

An investment plan must be created after taking into account the above considerations. And then that plan must be implemented, regularly reviewed, and adjusted when needed to meet the overall investment goals and objectives. In other words, there is a lot to consider, decide, implement, and review. How can a trustee possibly do all of that without a written investor policy statement? More importantly, *why* would a trustee do all of that without a written policy statement?

By having a written investment policy statement, the trustee can prove that they created and implemented a prudent investment plan. If notes are taken when meeting with the financial advisor, the trustee can prove that the investment plan was reviewed and any necessary changes were made to meet the investment goals. This type of proof is invaluable if the trustee is ever challenged for imprudent trust investing. And it has the added benefit of encouraging proper investing in the first place.

If you are a California trustee, do yourself a favor and create an investor policy statement with your financial advisor. If you are a California beneficiary, find out if your trustee has a written investor policy statement. If so, then you may be in good hands. If not, then be afraid, be very afraid . . .

In the case of Ben and Sam, Ben could have easily consulted a financial planner and created an investor policy statement. That plan should have included input from Sam since he was a named co-trustee. Once a plan was created, it could have been implemented to (1) benefit Sam, and (2) protect Ben from any future lawsuit for breach of his trustee duty to diversify trust assets. Sam's case is especially egregious considering he had a trust worth $9.5 million, yet Sam was living on $3,000 per month. Even a modest investment return of 3% per annum would have given Sam over $20,000 per month in income. Why was Ben being so abusive? Who knows? But Sam has the right to stand up and fight back for his rightful trust distributions.

Trust investment problems, or financial mismanagement, can wreak havoc on your trust estate. If you have questions about your trust investments, feel free to contact us at Albertson & Davidson, LLP. Our firm has handled hundreds of trust investment problems.

In Sam's case, he was the sole beneficiary, but what if Ben were treating another beneficiary more generously than Sam? The next topic of beneficiary abuse: a trustee's duty to treat the beneficiaries fairly and equally.

Chapter 5

Abuse Involving the Fair Treatment of Beneficiaries

In this chapter we will discuss a trustee's failure to treat beneficiaries fairly, especially where the trustee is also a trust beneficiary. We start with a basic understanding of the trust law that applies to this problem.

THE BASICS OF TREATING BENEFICIARIES FAIRLY UNDER CALIFORNIA LAW

The trustee has a duty to administer the trust solely in the interest of the beneficiaries. Under California Probate Code section 16003, if a trust has two or more beneficiaries, the trustee has a duty to deal impartially with them.

TREATING BENEFICIARIES FAIRLY HYPOTHETICAL: LUPE AS ABUSED BENEFICIARY

Let's consider a hypothetical situation to demonstrate the problems that arise and the options you have when confronted with a California trustee who fails to treat you fairly as a trust beneficiary. After the hypothetical, we will discuss trust diversification in terms of fair treatment of beneficiaries in more detail.

In 1995, Juanita and Rodolfo created a revocable living trust and transferred their home, a rental property, and their financial accounts into the trust. Juanita and Rodolfo have four children who are named as equal beneficiaries under the trust.

In 2001, Rodolfo had a severe stroke. Juanita could not care for Rodolfo alone, so their daughter, Lupe, moved into their home to help care for her father. Rodolfo died in 2004. Lupe continued to live in the family home rent-free with Juanita until Juanita's death in 2012. Lupe took care of her mother during the last several years of Juanita's life as Juanita's health slowly failed.

Upon Juanita's death, the total estate was worth $1.25 million. The family home was worth $250,000, the rental property was worth $200,000, and the financial accounts had $800,000 worth of cash, stocks, and bonds.

After Juanita died, her son Miguel took over as sole trustee of the trust. The four equal beneficiaries of the trust are Miguel and Lupe, along with their two brothers, Carlos and Damian.

Miguel was not happy that Lupe was allowed to live in the family home for so long without paying rent. He believed that Lupe should have to pay back rent to the trust. Lupe, however, has no job because she has been a full-time caregiver to her parents for many years. Lupe would like to keep the family home and continue living there.

Lupe argues that her share of the trust estate, after all trust expenses are paid, is worth at least $300,000 (one-fourth of $1.2 million), so she should be able to keep the family home worth $250,000 as part of her trust distribution. While the trustee could distribute the home to Lupe, Miguel refuses to do so because he also would like to keep the home and live in it himself.

Carlos and Damian do not care about the family home and are happy to allow either Miguel or Lupe to receive the home so long as Carlos and Damien receive their share of the trust estate in cash.

Miguel immediately starts eviction proceedings against Lupe to force her to move from the home. Lupe tells Miguel that she would need a cash distribution from the trust to at least rent a new place to move out. Miguel refuses to distribute any cash to Lupe until Lupe agrees to let Miguel have the house.

Lupe then offers to move into the rental property if Miguel will distribute that house to her as part of her trust share. Miguel refuses to do so because the rental home is under a long-term lease with the existing tenant and Miguel wants to keep the rental to produce income for the indefinite future.

Currently, there is enough cash on hand to pay Carlos and Damian their shares of the trust estate in cash. Carlos and Damian demand a cash distribution immediately. They believe that the fight over the real properties is none of their concern and they should not have to wait to get paid just because Lupe and Miguel cannot get along.

LUPE'S OPTIONS

It appears that Miguel is not treating the trust beneficiaries impartially. Miguel is refusing to separate his fiduciary duties as trustee from his personal desire to retain the trust's real estate. What can Lupe do to obtain her fair share of the trust estate and prevent Miguel from demanding back rent from her? Here are the options:

1. **Petition for instructions.** File a petition for instructions asking the court to order a distribution of the home to Lupe.

2. **Petition for accounting.** File a petition asking the court to order Miguel to prepare and file a trust accounting.

3. **Petition for removal.** File a petition to remove Miguel as trustee.

4. **Petition for damages.** File a petition for breach of trust seeking damages against Miguel.

5. **Petition to sell real estate.** File a petition for instructions asking the court to order the trustee to sell all trust assets and distribute the cash to the beneficiaries equally.

OUR EXPERT RECOMMENDATION

A sibling acting as trustee, especially a disgruntled sibling, is the typical starting point for beneficiary abuse. Here, Miguel is not being reasonable. He refuses to negotiate distribution of the home to Lupe, and he refuses to discuss the rental property. Instead, Miguel seems bent on revenge.

Option 3: as experienced trust and will attorneys, we would advise Lupe to petition for trustee removal. Miguel should be removed from office as trustee because he cannot treat the beneficiaries fairly. He seems to think that he is "in charge" and can do whatever he likes. But his duties as trustee are much different than that. As a trustee, Miguel must treat each of the beneficiaries fairly, which means that Miguel cannot benefit himself to the detriment of the other beneficiaries. As such, Miguel should be removed as trustee.

Option 1: removal takes time because the court must have a trial to determine the evidence for removal. In the meantime, we would advise Lupe to include option 1 and ask the court to order the trustee, either Miguel or his successor, to distribute the trust assets. We would ask the court to order a distribution of the home to Lupe. If Lupe wants the home, she might as well ask for it. The court may deny that request, but it is worth a try.

Option 5: it is also worth pursuing a petition asking that all the real estate be sold and the cash distributed equally. This would mean that Lupe does not get the home or the rental property, but it also means that Miguel won't get those assets either. In other words, we may be able to put pressure on Miguel by asking the court to force him to sell all the real estate. If Miguel truly wants to keep the rental property, then he will not like this request, and he may be more open to negotiating a distribution of the home to Lupe.

Keep in mind that sometimes you must take certain actions to help build leverage against the trustee. Lupe may not want all the real estate sold, but neither does Miguel. And if Lupe is willing to live with this result, but Miguel is not, then Lupe can gain some much-needed bargaining leverage by asking the court to sell everything.

Option 2: it may be premature to pursue a petition for accounting. If you know all the finances of the trust, there may be no need for an accounting. And since the accounting will likely cost the trust several tens of thousands of dollars to prepare, we would probably skip that for now. If we discover further facts that suggest some trust assets were misappropriated, then we may request an accounting at that time. For now, we would focus on getting the home distributed to Lupe.

Option 4: a petition for damages, the final option, is also premature. At this point, Miguel is causing a lot of problems, but he has not caused any damages yet. Unfortunately, a trustee is not liable for damages simply because they breached their duty as trustee. Instead, there must be some economic loss to the trust that was caused by the breach of trust. If a trustee is refusing to make a distribution, but the court then orders the trustee to distribute, there likely are no damages from a financial-loss perspective. Yes, you suffered mental anguish (or pain and suffering) due to the trustee's actions, but you cannot obtain damages from a trustee or trust for pain and suffering.

The Law of Diversifying Trust Assets Regarding Fair Treatment of Beneficiaries

Under California Probate Code section 16002, every California trustee has a duty to administer the trust solely in the interest of the beneficiaries. Further, Probate Code section 16003 states that if a trust has two or more beneficiaries, the trustee has a duty to (1) deal impartially with them, (2) treat them fairly in investing and managing trust property, and (3) consider any differing interests of the beneficiaries.

In other words, the trustee cannot play favorites. The trustee must act in a way that benefits ALL the beneficiaries as equally as possible. There are times when differing beneficial interests must be weighed. For example, investing trust assets to maximize income, but minimize growth, is a great strategy for the current income beneficiaries but could harm the future principal beneficiaries of the trust. To properly balance these differing beneficial interests, a trustee must invest for both income and growth.

Problems often arise where one beneficiary resides in a trust home rent-free. This is unfair to the other beneficiaries who have an interest in the same home. The trustee must collect rent, evict the beneficiary, or sell the home (or maybe do all three). Some action must be taken by the trustee to equalize the situation so that one beneficiary does not gain an unfair advantage over trust assets.

The guiding light for every trustee should be fairness. Whatever action best equalizes the beneficiaries so they all are benefitted, and no one is harmed, is the action the trustee must take. This is not optional; the trustee has an affirmative duty to treat each beneficiary fairly.

These duties sound simple, but many private trustees violate them because the trustees mistakenly assume that they are "in charge" and can do whatever they like. That is false. While a trustee is the manager of the trust estate, the job includes a host of legal duties and responsibilities. And the trustee duties are vastly different from what a person can do with their own assets. If the trustee has their own money and they want to benefit their children unequally, that's fine. But when a trustee is managing a trust estate, they do not have the freedom to play favorites. In accepting the job of trustee, the trustee is also agreeing to abide by the duties and responsibilities of a trustee.

INVESTMENT DECISIONS

The California Prudent Investor Act provides the rules a trustee must follow when investing trust assets. In part, the trustee must consider the differing interests of the beneficiaries when investing trust assets.

The most obvious differences come with the type of beneficial interests a trust can create. For example, one beneficiary may be entitled to receive all trust income monthly while a different beneficiary may be entitled to the principal of the trust once the income beneficiary dies. If the trustee invests with a view to only maximize income, then the principal assets may not grow in value, which would hurt the principal beneficiary. If the trustee invests with a view to only maximize the growth of the assets, then there may be no income generated to the detriment of the income beneficiary. Either of these investment strategies would be a violation of the trustee's duty to treat the beneficiaries impartially.

What action should the trustee take when dealing with differing beneficial interests? The trustee must have a well-thought-out and a well-documented investment plan. The trustee can consult with a financial advisor and create a written investor policy statement (referred to as an IPS). The IPS would outline the differing beneficial interests and then discuss an investment strategy that would balance both income and growth. The trustee can then implement the investment plan contained in the IPS and, more importantly, check on the plan every quarter with the financial advisor. By regularly checking up on the investment plan, any changes can be made due to changed circumstances in the investment portfolio.

The duty to treat beneficiaries impartially when investing trust assets is not hard to satisfy, but it does take some forethought, planning, and adjusting along the way. The trustee can hire professional advisors, which is where a good financial advisor should be used. There is no reason to leave trust investments to chance or guess work. A trustee should devise a good investment plan, write the plan down in an IPS, and then implement the plan. This protects the trustee from being sued, and it protects the beneficiaries from being treated unfairly.

FIGHTS AMONG BENEFICIARIES

Sometimes trust beneficiaries don't get along (imagine that), especially where the beneficiaries are siblings with a long history of family discord. There are many issues that beneficiaries may fight over. It could be a disagreement over the interpretation of a trust provision or arguing over who receives the family home. Sometimes beneficiaries argue over seemingly mundane issues, such as who will receive the original family photographs or who will receive the heirloom teapot. These "mundane" issues can be the biggest fights of all because even though the monetary value is low, the sentimental value can be priceless.

Whatever the issue may be, the trustee has a duty NOT to take sides in disputes among beneficiaries. This is true even in disputes concerning trust amendments. So long as the validity of the trust itself is not being attacked, any dispute between beneficiaries requires impartiality on the part of the trustee.

What if the trustee is also a beneficiary? That gets complicated because the trustee is essentially wearing two hats—one as trustee (requiring impartiality) and one as beneficiary. The best practice in this scenario is for the trustee/beneficiary to hire two different lawyers. One lawyer would represent the trustee/beneficiary as trustee and help the trustee remain impartial. This lawyer can be paid from the trust estate because they are providing services to the trust. The trustee can provide any helpful information to the parties and to the court, but cannot take an adversarial role in the fight.

The other lawyer would represent the trustee/beneficiary as a beneficiary. This lawyer must be paid by the beneficiary individually, and they could advocate on behalf of the beneficiary. In other words, the trustee/beneficiary can take sides in a fight, provided that they do so as an individual beneficiary only. That means no trust assets or resources can be used to fund the beneficiary's fight.

This may all sound complicated, but it is crucially important if the trustee/beneficiary wishes to abide by their legal duties and remain impartial as a trustee. Where a trustee/beneficiary fails to take the actions described above, they risk being found in breach of trust, which could cause them to be removed and surcharged for damages.

Remaining impartial is not always easy. Many trustees, even those who are not beneficiaries, want to take sides with the beneficiaries with whom they agree, but that is strictly forbidden. The trustee has an affirmative duty to rise above the fray and remain impartial in all beneficiary fights.

CURRENT VS. REMAINDER BENEFICIARIES

Most trusts have different layers of beneficiaries to consider. Current vs. remainder beneficiaries are the most common. For example, when a bypass trust is created, the surviving spouse is the current beneficiary. Income and principal of the trust are typically distributed to the surviving spouse for their health, education, maintenance, or support. Once the surviving spouse dies, the remainder beneficiaries (usually the children) receive whatever is left in the bypass trust estate.

In managing the bypass trust assets, the trustee has a duty to consider both the current and remainder beneficiaries. That means all management and investment decisions must balance these competing interests. Naturally, the remainder beneficiaries would prefer that the assets are invested for growth and that NO distributions are made from the trust. Whereas the surviving spouse would prefer investments geared toward income with liberal distributions of income and principal being made.

The trustee must balance these competing interests and decide how best to treat all the beneficiaries fairly. Bypass trusts are just one example of a trust with different layers of beneficiaries. The same is true for marital trusts, children's trusts, any trust that holds assets for one person or group of people currently but then distributes the assets to a different person or group of people later.

As with investing, the best course to ensure a trustee satisfies their duty to treat beneficiaries fairly is to create a written plan. For investing, the trustee can use an IPS to create and implement a proper investment plan. For managing other trust assets or making trust distributions, written documentation is also critical. For example, the trustee can ask the current beneficiary to provide a list of their needs in writing, or the trustee can meet with the current beneficiary and create a list of needs together. The trustee can then obtain whatever supporting documentation they feel is appropriate to justify the list of needs. Finally, the trustee can make the distributions. A thorough and well-documented plan of action helps protect the trustee from future attack and helps ensure the beneficiaries are treated fairly.

As with all duties of a trustee, a little forethought, documentation, and planning goes a long way to satisfying trustee duties. Trustees who take the time to execute their duties properly are the best trustees you can have.

In the case of Miguel, he was simply acting unfairly. A trustee must treat each beneficiary equally and fairly. A trustee is not allowed to play favorites. Even though Miguel was mad at Lupe, he had no right to use his position as trustee to take out his revenge against her. Luckily, Lupe can stand up and fight for her beneficial rights in court. Miguel can try to abuse Lupe, but Miguel's abuse cannot continue once he must answer for his actions before a judge.

Intra-family fights fuel many trust disputes. With Miguel, the fight was for real estate, but similar disputes can arise with family businesses as well, which is the subject of the next chapter.

Chapter 6

Abuse Involving the Passing of a Family Business

In this chapter we will discuss problems that arise with family-owned businesses. We start with a basic understanding of the law we will apply to this problem.

THE BASICS OF CALIFORNIA INHERITANCE FOR MARRIED COUPLES

Under Probate Code section 6401, where a married person dies and has no will or trust, all their community property passes to the surviving spouse. Community property refers to property jointly owned by a married couple. The surviving spouse is also entitled to either one-third or one-half of the deceased spouse's separate property, depending on how many children the deceased spouse had living at time of death. Separate property refers to property owned by only one of a married couple. This allocation is officially termed an "intestate distribution scheme."

This intestate distribution scheme can be changed by using a will, trust, joint titling (such as joint tenants), or beneficiary designation (as used in life insurance policies).

Family Businesses Hypothetical: Simon and Todd as Abused Beneficiaries

Let's consider a hypothetical situation to demonstrate the problems that arise and the options you have when confronted with a California intestate distribution of community property and separate property. After the hypothetical, we will discuss inheritance of assets between married couples in more detail.

Walter and Patty married in January 1998. They each had previously been married, and Walter has two sons from his prior marriage, Simon and Todd. A year after marrying Patty, Walter created a business, and both sons worked in that business for the last eighteen years. Walter paid Simon and Todd a reasonable salary for the work they did.

In February 2017, Walter died. The business grew over time and was worth $3 million at the time of Walter's death. Both sons helped grow the business substantially, and Walter considered his sons to be equal partners in the business. Walter said many times that the business would pass to Simon and Todd, and he told them both they were equal owners. Unfortunately, Walter never took any steps to change the actual ownership of the business to his sons—the business was legally owned 100% by Walter at the time of his death.

Walter never created a will or a trust. He owned a home with Patty that was titled in their names as joint tenants with right of survivorship. The home is worth $1 million. He also had a bank account held jointly with Patty and an investment portfolio worth $500,000 titled jointly with Patty.

After Walter's death, Simon and Todd tried to change the authorized signers on the business checking account from Walter to Simon and Todd. But the bank refused to do so because Simon and Todd were not legal owners of the business. The bank told them they needed a court order. Simon and Todd then consulted an attorney who told them the business had to pass through probate to be transferred, meaning there had to be a court-supervised transfer of assets in probate court. So, Simon and Todd hired the lawyer to handle the court-supervised transfer of assets (referred to as probate) for Walter's estate, so the business could pass to them.

Meanwhile, Patty also consulted a lawyer. The lawyer helped Patty secure her home, bank account, and the investment portfolio in Patty's sole name since she was a joint owner. Patty then asked about who would receive the business. Patty's lawyer pointed out that the business was not held in a trust or governed by a will, so the business would pass under California intestacy laws, meaning laws that address estates that aren't governed by a will or trust. Under California intestacy laws, all the community property would pass to Patty alone. In other words, there was a good chance Patty would receive the entire business through probate. Even if the business were considered separate property, Patty would be entitled to one-third of the business under California intestate laws. Patty's lawyer was not certain if the business would be considered community property or separate property by the court, but Patty had a claim to the business, or a portion of the business, either way.

After Simon and Todd filed a petition for probate, Patty filed a competing petition claiming sole ownership of the business. Simon and Todd became understandably upset. Plus, they later learned that if the business was classified as community property, then it would pass entirely to Patty. And if the business was classified as separate property, then Patty would receive one-third of the business. Either way, Simon and Todd may lose a substantial amount of money.

SIMON AND TODD'S OPTIONS

It appears that Patty has a good argument that she should receive the entire business from Walter's estate. What can Simon and Todd do to protect their rights to the family business? Here are the options:

1. **Contract to make a will.** Simon and Todd file to enforce the agreement their father made to leave them the business.

2. **Find a holographic will.** Search through Walter's files to see if he ever wrote down his intentions in his own handwriting (that's called a holographic will).

3. **File a creditor's claim.** Simon and Todd assert that they had a general partnership with their father, and they are entitled to the business as general partners.

4. Negotiate with Patty. **Simon and Todd can negotiate with Patty** in an attempt to settle the matter with her voluntarily.

OUR EXPERT RECOMMENDATION

Simon and Todd have received a rude awakening. Despite their many years of service to the business, they may now have lost the asset to Patty.

Option 1: as practiced litigators in this area, the first action we would recommend Simon and Todd take is to assert a contract to make a will. It seems that Walter made many statements that he intended to leave the business to his sons. These statements, taken alone, are not enough to have a contract to make a will. But if these statements were made in exchange for the sons working in the business and helping build it up, then that could be an enforceable agreement.

In other words, a contract to make a will is no different from any other contract; it must have consideration. In this context, consideration refers to something bargained for and received by a promisor from a promisee. Common types of consideration include real estate or personal property, a return promise, some act, or a forbearance. If Dad promised to leave the business to his sons as a gift, that is not a contract because there is no consideration for that promise. If, however, Dad promised to leave the business to his sons, and in exchange the sons agreed to take less pay and/or pass up other work opportunities to help grow the business, then that could be an enforceable agreement. In the latter case, the sons gave something in exchange for Walter's promise to leave them the business—that's a contract.

Unfortunately, it does not appear that the contract was in writing, which makes it harder to prove and enforce. Also, the sons were paid a reasonable salary for their services. Patty's lawyer could argue that the sons did not give up anything in exchange for Walter's promise because the sons were paid a salary. As such, there was no consideration and no contract. These are hurdles the sons will have to confront to succeed on their contract to make a will claim.

Option 2: finding a holographic will is always a good idea. A holographic will is written in the handwriting of the testator and signed by them—no witnesses are required. This is different from a type-written will, which requires two witnesses to be valid. You may be surprised at the types of writings that can be considered holographic wills. For example, a letter could be a holographic will if it is written in the testator's handwriting. We have seen cases where a sticky note was deemed a holographic will, a note card, a page from a notebook, and a napkin—you name it. Anything that is handwritten by the testator and expresses their intent to create a will could be a holographic will.

Here, perhaps Walter wrote a note saying, "On my death I leave my business to Simon and Todd." If he signed that note, then it could be a holographic will. It expresses Walter's intent to create a will, it states his intentions, and it is in Walter's own handwriting. All the ingredients are present for a holographic will.

As a result, don't just assume there is no will because there is not a formal, type-written will. Look through the handwritten material of the decedent and see if they ever wrote down their intentions. You may find a will where you least expect it.

Even if there is a holographic will, Patty still may have a claim to half of the business as her share of the community property. Walter could make a will leaving his half of the community property to his sons, but Walter could not leave Patty's share to Simon and Todd without Patty's consent. As such, a holographic will, even if found, may only help the sons as to half of the business.

Option 3: assuming there is no holographic will, then it may be good to file a creditor's claim. Simon and Todd could file a creditor's claim based on their partnership with Walter. In other words, even though Simon and Todd were not legal owners of the business, they all agreed that they were partners. General partnerships need not be officially created with the Secretary of State's office. People can simply agree to be partners. In fact, general partnerships don't have to be written at all. You can have an oral agreement to be a general partnership.

Naturally, creating a general partnership by oral agreement is a terrible idea because how do you prove the partnership existed? It can be difficult, but if you have the proof, then your partnership can be enforced.

One of the hallmarks of a general partnership is that the partners must share in the losses and gains of the business. If Simon and Todd received a salary and did not share in the losses and gains of the business, then they will have difficulty establishing a general partnership. If, however, Simon and Todd were paid a percentage of the profits and were not paid when the profits went down or were negative, then the general partnership argument may be stronger. In any event, it would be advantageous to assert a general partnership, provided that there are some facts to support that claim.

Option 4: negotiation with Patty may be a better option in this case than it is in most cases. The reason: Simon and Todd run the business while Patty does not. In fact, Patty may have no idea how to run the business if she has not been involved in that business over the last ten years. For example, perhaps Patty was working in her own career during that time and did not pay much attention to how Walter ran the business. Meanwhile, both Simon and Todd would have an intimate knowledge of how the business is run given their involvement in it over the past ten years.

Many small businesses lose their value once the owner/operator leaves. If Simon and Todd leave the business, the value of the business may drop or even become worthless. If that is the case, then Simon and Todd would be in a much stronger position to negotiate with Patty. In other words, Patty either must cut a deal with Simon and Todd, or Simon and Todd will leave the business.

Obviously, option 4 depends on the circumstances of the business and Patty's ability to run the business if Simon and Todd leave. Hopefully, the parties can come to a voluntary agreement and save themselves many thousands in attorneys' fees and costs. Most people are not able to do that, unfortunately.

If the parties are not able to resolve this matter voluntarily, then they have a long, difficult fight on their hands that likely will last for a few years.

Community Property vs. Separate Property

Under California law, the surviving spouse inherits all community property unless there is a trust or will that says otherwise (see Probate Code section 6401).

The surviving spouse will receive a portion of separate property as well. Under California law, if a decedent dies and has one child, then the child receives half of the separate property, and the surviving spouse receives the other half. If the decedent has two or more children, then the spouse receives a third of the separate property and the rest is divided equally among the children. Either way, the surviving spouse will receive a portion of the separate property.

These basic rules of intestate inheritance apply to property held in the name of a decedent who dies without a trust or will. There are other ways to pass assets, such as jointly titled assets, for example, but absent some other arrangement the inheritance rules described above will apply.

Unfortunately, many people are surprised to learn of these inheritance rules. You might think that you should receive your parent's property at death, but the law says otherwise. In fact, most property will pass to the surviving spouse—all the community property plus either a third or a half of the separate property—unless a trust or will is created. That could be a substantial amount of property passing to a surviving spouse.

THE IMPORTANCE OF WELL-DRAFTED TRUSTS AND WILLS

A WORD ON TRUSTS

The best way to avoid unintended consequences is to create a well-drafted trust or will that provides for your wishes. A trust will control all assets funded into the name of the trust by the decedent prior to death. For example, you might create a trust and transfer title to your home to the name of the trust. Once this occurs, the trust terms will govern how that home is distributed after your death.

The great thing about trusts is that they are highly flexible. You can draft almost anything you can imagine into a trust—provided it is legal. From a more practical perspective, you can add trust provisions that allow a surviving spouse to live in a home until their death and then transfer ownership of the property to your children. Or maybe the surviving spouse has the right to occupy your home for a couple of years and then ownership passes to your children. Or maybe the home is sold, and a cash payout goes to the surviving spouse, or whatever else you can imagine.

In other words, a trust will allow you to arrange your affairs the way you want them. Unfortunately, many people refuse to use a trust. They think that things will just work out. Or maybe they think the surviving spouse will take care of their children. Whatever people without trusts may think, things rarely go as planned, especially when the plans have not been made to begin with by failing to create a valid trust.

A WORD ON WILLS

A will can also be a helpful device when used properly. For starters, a will can be used to determine who will receive your property when you die. And you can even stipulate in your will that assets must be held in trust for some length of time. The difference between trusts and wills is that wills require a court supervised transfer of assets (called probate), whereas trusts can transfer assets without court supervision. But that is not the worst thing in the world. Probate allows for court supervision of the distribution of your assets. And a proper accounting by your personal representative must be provided before the estate can be closed. Sometimes a little court oversight can be helpful.

Unfortunately, wills only apply to any assets held in your name at the time of your death. If you have assets in a trust, then the will does not control those assets—the trust does. And if you have any assets titled in joint tenancy with another person (or other people), then the asset will pass automatically to the surviving joint tenant(s) and your will does not apply. In other words, the way in which your assets are titled ultimately determines whether or not your will controls them. That means the titling of your assets is just as important as the creation of your will if you want your will to work properly.

For example, a person could create a will that mandates all assets be passed equally to their children upon their death. But after creation of the will, the person then adds their son as a joint tenant on all their bank accounts thinking the son will help pay the bills. While you may think that the son will share the assets with the other children after death, there is no obligation to do so. The son has the right, as the surviving joint tenant, to keep everything in the joint accounts. And the will does not control the joint accounts because the joint titling trumps the will. It can be a complete mess when people fail to plan properly.

A Word on Survivors Trusts, Bypass Trusts, and Marital Trusts

Many married people have created trusts that have new trusts created after the first spouse dies. These new trusts are called sub-trusts because they are created under the terms of the original trust and they each receive a portion of the trust assets after the first spouse dies.

In years past, these sub-trusts were created for estate tax purposes. But as the federal estate tax limit has increased substantially (in 2017 a single person could pass up to $5.49 million without estate tax; and married couples could double that with $10.98 million), the utility of these sub-trusts has diminished greatly for tax planning.

But sub-trusts have another benefit—control. By using sub-trusts, the decedent spouse could ensure that their property would be held for the benefit of the surviving spouse during their lifetime but not give the surviving spouse control over the assets. In other words, the first spouse to die would be ensured that the assets would ultimately pass to their children, not to the surviving spouse or to the surviving spouse's children.

Commonly, people simply leave their assets to the surviving spouse under the assumption that the survivor either will not change the estate plan, or thinking the survivor will "do the right thing." The "right thing" can be far more subjective than you think, especially when you are in the shoes of the children.

The control aspect of sub-trusts is often overlooked or underappreciated. Control is especially important when spouses have children from past marriages. All too often, the surviving spouse does not want to benefit the deceased spouse's children. By having an element of control in your trust, you can help ensure that assets pass to the right people at the right time.

THE OMITTED SPOUSE

Under Probate Code section 21610, your spouse has the right to a portion of your estate if you marry after creation of a trust or will. In other words, if you have a will or trust created, and then you marry, your new spouse will receive a share of your assets even if that was not your intent. This is referred to as an omitted spouse.

The omitted spouse rule does not apply if the will or trust is created after marriage. It also does not apply if you clearly state in your will or trust that you do not intend to leave anything to your spouse. That means you have to amend your estate plan if you are planning to marry. If you fail to do so, then your spouse automatically receives a portion of your assets.

This can be a trap for people who do not know about omitted spouse rules. You may think that your will or trust that leaves everything to your children will still apply if you later marry. But that is not true. The only way to ensure your existing plan will still apply after you marry is to amend the plan to reference your marriage and state how you want your assets distributed after the marriage. You still have the right to leave your half of the community property, and all of your separate property, to anyone you like (it does not have to be your spouse). But you can only do so by changing your plan after your marriage.

JOINTLY TITLED ASSETS

Jointly titled assets have rules of their own. Jointly titled assets are not governed by wills or trusts. For example, if you have a bank account with your spouse as joint tenant with right of survivorship, then that account will pass to the surviving spouse automatically upon your death. You may have a different intent expressed in your will or trust, but that will not apply.

The same is true of your home. A home titled in joint tenancy or in community property with right of survivorship will automatically pass title to your surviving spouse upon your death regardless of anything stated in your will or trust.

This changes if your home is titled in the name of your trust. Once an asset is titled in your trust, then the trust provisions will control that asset. It all comes down to how assets are titled. Once you know that, then you can determine how the assets will pass at death. Don't assume that a will or trust controls the passage of all assets. That may not be the case depending on how the assets are titled.

In the case of Walter, he made a big mess of his family-owned business by not properly planning for the transfer of that asset. Walter said that his sons were joint owners, but he never documented that in writing. And Simon and Todd spent years working in the family business without ever asking for documentation of their business ownership. It is not uncommon for family businesses to be less formal than non-family-owned businesses, but the consequences of being less formal can be substantial. For Simon and Todd, they can stand up and fight for their share of the family business, but it will not be an easy fight. Patty has substantial rights, and it remains unclear who will walk away with the business. Anytime you enter into a messy case with conflicting legal rights, you are assured of only one thing: no one will be happy with the ultimate result.

Now that you know something about beneficiary abuse with a family-owned business and the other areas of abuse covered in the first five chapters, the next step is learning how to stop the abuse, which we address in the next, and final, chapter of this book.

Chapter 7

How to Stop the Abuse

If you are being abused by a bad trustee or a bad executor, you are not alone. Every day thousands of people are forced to fight for their inheritances. As a beneficiary, you may have no power, and you may have no money, but you do have rights. Using your legal rights as a beneficiary, you can turn the tables on your bad trustee, but you have to know what those rights are and how to enforce them.

The good news is that trustees owe substantial fiduciary duties to beneficiaries, while beneficiaries owe no duties to trustees. Trustee duties are a one-way street. You can use that to your advantage by demanding the trustee adhere to their fiduciary duties. And you don't have to worry about the trustee forcing you to do the same because you owe no duties to the trustee.

Hopefully, this book gave you some idea of what your rights are and the possible ways you can enforce those rights. Now the work is up to you. If you want to enforce the rights you have, you must take action. No one else is going to protect your legal rights for you. So stand up and assert the rights you have as a trust beneficiary. It is not easy, but it will be worthwhile once you get the inheritance you deserve.

NOW WHAT?

What should you do if you have a trust distribution problem? We recommend you consider taking the following steps:

STEP 1: SEND A WRITTEN REQUEST IN WRITING.

You have to ask for what you want from the trustee in writing, but you don't have to use any magic language. It does not take a law degree to send a letter or email to your trustee listing what you want. Here is a sample demand letter to a trustee who refuses to make a trust distribution:

[The date]

Mr. Trustee
1234 Main Street
Los Angeles, California
Re: Trust Distribution and Trust Accounting

Dear Mr. Trustee:

I am demanding that you provide the following documents to me for a proper assessment of accounts. Additionally, I am hereby demanding that you provide me with a formal accounting of your actions in administering the trust from the date you initially became trustee to the present date. To the extent you have any documents responsive to this demand that pertain to actions undertaken by you as trustee, please produce all such documents. Finally, if there are any other trustees of the trust, we hereby further demand that they provide us with a formal accounting of their actions in administering the trust from the date they initially became trustee to the present date.

1. Demand for documents pertaining to the trust estate.

This letter is a formal request for you to provide me with the following:

- All trust documents pertaining to the trust, including without limitation amendments, and restatements;

- All last will and testaments pertaining to _____, including without limitation amendments, and codicils;

- All durable powers of attorney and/or powers of attorney pertaining to _____;

- Any and all information pertaining to all the trust's assets (which includes but is not limited to all documentation pertaining to the trust's real and personal property), including without limitation all payments made for repairs on real and personal property;

- Any and all information pertaining to rental income received from real properties held by the trust and any expenses for rental properties paid by the trust;

- Any and all information pertaining to the trust's assets, which were allocated to the bypass trust.

- Any and all information pertaining to the trust's assets, which were allocated to the survivor's trust.

- Any and all information pertaining to all the trust's financial accounts as well as all financial accounts at any financial institution;

- Any and all information pertaining to tax returns or property taxes, which involved the trust's assets;

- Any and all invoices for attorneys' fees paid from the trust's assets;

- An accounting of all trustee fees paid from the trust;

- An accounting of all distributions made to any of the trust's beneficiaries;

- An accounting of all disbursements made in excess of $1,000.00 by any trustee;

- A formal trust accounting under Probate Code sections 16062 and 16063 to be filed with the court in accordance with Probate Code section 1060, from the date you became trustee to present;

- Your plan for making distributions under the trust;

- Copies of all lease agreements, rent receipts, listing agreements, appraisals, offers, and purchase agreements made on any and all of the trust's real property, including but not limited t real property known as _____, and real property known as _____.

As you may be aware, under California law you have substantial duties as a trustee of the trust, which includes but is not limited to the following:

2. Duty to administer the trust.

On acceptance of the trust, the trustee has a duty to administer the trust according to the trust instrument except to the extent the trust instrument provides otherwise (Prob. Code § 16000).

Confirm the following based on the terms of the trust instrument:

- That bank accounts have been established for the trust; and

- The balance in the trust's bank accounts.

3. Duty to report information about the trust on request and to account to beneficiaries.

The trustee shall report to the beneficiary by providing requested information to the beneficiary relating to the administration of the trust relevant to the beneficiary's interest (Prob. Code § 16061). The trustee also has a duty to account to each beneficiary of the trust (Prob. Code § 16062).

Under Probate Code section 1060, an accounting furnished by the trustee and filed with the court must contain:

- The period covered by the accounting;

- The property on hand at the beginning of the period covered by the account, which shall be the value of the property initially received by the trustee if this is the first account;

- The value of any assets received during the period of the accounting, which are not assets on hand as of the commencement of the administration of the estate;

- The amount of any receipts of income or principal;

- Net income from a trade or business;

- Gains or sales;

- The amount of disbursements, excluding disbursements for a trade or business or distributions;

- Loss on sales;

- Net loss from trade or business;

- Distributions to beneficiaries; and

- Property on hand at the end of the accounting period, stated as its carry value.

In addition, the accounting must include supporting schedules in accordance with Probate Code sections 1062 and 1063.

Please confirm that you will provide a formal probate accounting of your acts as trustee of the trust.

4. Duty to provide information, and if not, be compelled.

The trustee, on the request of a beneficiary or an heir, must provide a copy of the terms of the trust (Prob. Code, § 16060.7; Prob. Code, § 17200 (b)(7)(A)).

If the trustee fails to provide the requested information about the trust in accordance with Probate Code section 16061 within sixty days after the beneficiary's reasonable written request, and the beneficiary has not received the requested information from the trustee within the six months preceding the request, then a beneficiary of the trust may petition the court to compel the trustee to provide such information (Prob. Code, § 17200 (b)(7)(A) through (C)).

Please confirm that you will provide me with a formal accounting.

5. Conclusion

Please notify me no later than _____, 2018 whether you intend to provide the information and documents requested in this letter. If I do not hear from you by close of business on _____, 2018, I will assume that you have no intention of cooperating in this matter and will apply to the court for relief.

That's a heck of a letter isn't it? You can use it all you want, just copy it into your letter or email and send it off. The California Probate Code requires that you give trustees sixty days in which to respond to a demand for information and/or accounting. By sending this letter, you can get the sixty-day period running. There is no need to send the letter by certified mail (if you mail it). Just keep track of the date (either by writing it down or copying the date of the mail stamp if you mail the letter at the post office) you sent the letter to trigger the sixty-day requirement for the trustee to respond. If you do not receive what you ask for by sixty days, then you can file a petition in court. If you do receive what you ask for, then you are one of the lucky few who don't have to go to court.

STEP 2: FILE YOUR PETITION IN COURT.

If the demand letter does not work, then you must file in court to receive the help you need. Can you file in court without a lawyer? "He who represents himself has a fool for a client," so said Abraham Lincoln. That may be true in many cases, but is it true with probate petitions? Perhaps. It depends on the amount of time and effort you can spare to learn the ways of the probate court.

The benefit to hiring a lawyer to help you file a petition in probate court is that we lawyers have done your same case a thousand times before. We know the drill, you don't. If you have time on your hands and want to learn the nuances of probate law and procedures for filing in probate court, then you could file on your own. Obviously, most people don't choose to go it alone without legal help.

If you decide to file on your own, you may want to find a local law library. Most counties in California have a public legal library that anyone can use. The library will have all the reference materials you need to look up the statutes and case law required to file your petition in court. And many of the libraries also have forms you can review or use to file your own petition.

If you are going to hire a lawyer, then try to find someone who has experience in probate court. Probate is a unique area of the law, and it helps to have some experience handling trust cases in probate court. For example, our firm has handled hundreds of cases regarding beneficiary abuse (in fact, we coined the phrase "beneficiary abuse"). Albertson & Davidson, LLP, has obtained over $100 million in verdicts and settlements for our clients, representing inheritances that would have been lost without our help. We have a team of trial lawyers that focus exclusively on trust and will litigation issues. And we enjoy helping people fight against abuse at a time when they need it the most: after the death of a family member, usually. Trusts and wills are a complicated area of the law, and we help cut through that confusion, stop beneficiary abuse, and obtain rightful inheritances for beneficiaries.

STEP 3: MAKE SURE YOU RECEIVE A PROPER TRUST ACCOUNTING.

Beneficiaries have a right to receive trust financial information and trust accountings. You know when you have a proper trust accounting because it will describe every financial transaction that occurred from start to finish—much like a bank account statement. The following is a sample trust accounting that would be proper for a trustee to provide to a beneficiary:

Summary of Account

Case Number:

Report dates: From 09/01/2013 to 08/31/2014

Charges:

Amount of Assets on Hand		
(per Third Account Current)		
Cash Assets	$38,138.44	
Non-Cash Assets	$468,913.85	
Total Assets		$507,052.29
Non-Principal Cash Receipts (Schedule A)		$339,568.70
Gain on Sale (Schedule B)		$1,855.48
Total Charges:		**$848,476.47**

Credits:

Non-Principal Cash Disbursements (Schedule C)		$76,509.77
Loss on Sales (Schedule D)		$446.83
Property on hand (Schedule E)		
Cash Assets	$92,554.37	
Non-Cash Assets	$678,965.50	
Total Assets		$771,519.87
Total Credits:		**$848,476.47**

Schedule A-1
Assets on Hand
Case Number:

At the Beginning of the Accounting Period
September 1, 2013

Description	Carrying Value
Cash Assets	
1 Community Bank Personal Interest Account Account No:	$2,839.14
2 Security Bank Checking Account Account No:	$11,206.21
3 Security Bank Money Market Account No:	$24,092.52
4 Raymond James Brokerage Account Account No:	$0.57
Total Cash Assets	**$38,138.44**

Non-Cash Assets

2 Raymond James
Brokerage Account
Account No:

Schedule A-1
Assets on Hand
Case Number:

At the Beginning of the Accounting Period
September 1, 2013

	Description	Carrying Value
a	Blackrock Floating Rate Income 1093.634 shares	$11,417.98
b	Blackrock Global Long/Short Credit Fund 1069.684 shares	$11,274.58
c	Blackrock GNMA Portfolio 1125.913 shares	$11,402.28
d	Blackrock High Yield Bond 1414.560 shares	$11,529.92
e	Blackrock Strategic Inc. Opportunities 2984.038 shares	$30,287.46
3	Single Family Residence located at APN No.	$365,000.00
4	Refrigerator	$2,227.06
5	Furniture	$2,256.72
6	TV	$511.91
7	Promissory Note for A.D. (Unpaid Balance)	$23,005.94
	Total Non-Cash Assets	**$468,913.85**

Schedule A-1
Assets on Hand

Case Number:

At the Beginning of the Accounting Period
September 1, 2013

Description	Carrying Value
Total All Assets	**$507,052.29**

Schedule A
Receipts during Period, by Category
Case Number:

Report dates: From 09/01/2013 to 08/31/2014

Payor or Source of Receipt *Date of receipt/Description/Amount*	*Principal* *Amount*	*Non-Principal* *Amount*

Dividends

Raymond James
Brokerage Account
Account No:

<u>Blackrock Floating Rate Income</u>

09/03/13	Dividend paid	$30.00
10/01/13	Dividend paid	$29.18
11/01/13	Dividend paid	$34.41
12/02/13	Dividend paid	$36.79
01/02/14	Dividend paid	$35.11
02/03/14	Dividend paid	$34.94
03/03/14	Dividend paid	$33.75
04/01/14	Dividend paid	$36.98
05/01/14	Dividend paid	$36.53
06/02/14	Dividend paid	$38.80
07/01/14	Dividend paid	$42.26
08/01/14	Dividend paid	$1.35
		$390.10

<u>Blackrock Global Long/Short Credit Fund</u>

09/03/13	Dividend paid	$0.37
10/01/13	Dividend paid	$0.72
11/01/13	Dividend paid	$4.02
12/02/13	Dividend paid	$3.89
01/02/14	Dividend paid	$5.40

Schedule A
Receipts during Period, by Category
Case Number:

Report dates: From 09/01/2013 to 08/31/2014

		Principal Amount	*Non-Principal Amount*
02/03/14	Dividend paid		$5.88
03/03/14	Dividend paid		$9.27
04/01/14	Dividend paid		$6.80
05/01/14	Dividend paid		$5.94
06/02/14	Dividend paid		$5.87
07/01/14	Dividend paid		$7.54
			$55.70

Blackrock GNMA Portfolio

09/03/13	Dividend paid		$22.51
10/03/13	Dividend paid		$23.24
			$45.75

Blackrock High Yield Bond

09/03/13	Dividend paid		$50.32
10/01/13	Dividend paid		$47.47
11/01/13	Dividend paid		$60.27
12/02/13	Dividend paid		$58.73
12/23/13	Dividend paid		$192.27
12/23/13	Dividend paid		$16.30
01/02/14	Dividend paid		$64.27
02/03/14	Dividend paid		$68.73
03/03/14	Dividend paid		$61.79
04/01/14	Dividend paid		$65.44
05/01/14	Dividend paid		$54.62
06/02/14	Dividend paid		$56.46
07/01/14	Dividend paid		$59.79

Schedule A
Receipts during Period, by Category
Case Number:

Report dates: From 09/01/2013 to 08/31/2014

		Principal Amount	Non-Principal Amount
08/01/14	Dividend paid		$2.02
			$858.48

Blackrock Strategic Inc. Opportunities

09/03/13	Dividend paid		$25.83
10/01/13	Dividend paid		$28.33
11/01/13	Dividend paid		$29.58
12/02/13	Dividend paid		$28.77
01/02/14	Dividend paid		$26.11
02/03/14	Dividend paid		$23.41
03/03/14	Dividend paid		$35.38
04/01/14	Dividend paid		$39.44
05/01/14	Dividend paid		$43.63
06/02/14	Dividend paid		$43.29
07/01/14	Dividend paid		$39.89
08/01/14	Dividend paid		$1.63
			$365.29

Lord Abbett Bond Debenture

08/01/14	Dividend paid		$71.96
08/01/14	Dividend paid		$16.05
08/01/14	Dividend paid		$39.63
			$127.64

Schedule A
Receipts during Period, by Category
Case Number:

Report dates: From 09/01/2013 to 08/31/2014

		Principal Amount	Non-Principal Amount
Pimco Total Return			
08/01/14	Dividend paid		$32.18
Templeton Global Bond Fund			
08/18/14	Dividend paid		$54.69
Vanguard High Yield Corporate			
08/01/14	Dividend paid		$33.58
Interest			
Security Bank Checking Account Account No:			
09/30/13	Interest earned		$1.00
10/31/13	Interest earned		$1.00
11/29/13	Interest earned		$10.34
12/31/13	Interest earned		$0.57
01/31/14	Interest earned		$1.74
02/28/14	Interest earned		$1.80
03/31/14	Interest earned		$1.87
04/30/14	Interest earned		$1.62
05/30/14	Interest earned		$2.05
06/30/14	Interest earned		$1.31
07/31/14	Interest earned		$1.15

Schedule A
Receipts during Period, by Category
Case Number:

Report dates: From 09/01/2013 to 08/31/2014

		Principal Amount	*Non-Principal Amount*
08/29/14	Interest earned		$0.57
			$25.02

Security Bank
Money Market
Account No:

09/30/13	Interest earned		$1.98
10/31/13	Interest earned		$1.84
11/29/13	Interest earned		$6.48
12/31/13	Interest earned		$18.95
01/31/14	Interest earned		$11.99
02/28/14	Interest earned		$9.61
03/31/14	Interest earned		$10.65
04/30/14	Interest earned		$10.30
05/30/14	Interest earned		$10.65
06/30/14	Interest earned		$10.31
07/31/14	Interest earned		$10.65
08/29/14	Interest earned		$10.65
			$114.06

Security Bank
CDARs
Account No:

02/27/14	CDARs interest		$24.66
05/29/14	CDARs interest		$24.94
			$49.60

Schedule A
Receipts during Period, by Category
Case Number:

Report dates: From 09/01/2013 to 08/31/2014

		Principal Amount	*Non-Principal Amount*
Raymond James			
Brokerage Account			
Account No:			
05/30/14	Interest earned		$0.16
06/30/14	Interest earned		$1.64
07/31/14	Interest earned		$1.20
08/29/14	Interest earned		$0.01
			$3.01

Annuity Payments

09/13/13	GLAIC payment		$3,049.19
10/15/13	GLAIC payment		$3,049.19
11/15/13	GLAIC payment		$3,049.19
12/13/13	GLAIC payment		$3,140.67
01/15/14	GLAIC payment		$3,140.67
02/14/14	GLAIC payment		$3,140.67
03/14/14	GLAIC payment		$3,140.67
04/14/14	GLAIC payment		$3,140.67
05/15/14	GLAIC payment		$3,140.67
06/13/14	GLAIC payment		$3,140.67
07/14/14	GLAIC payment		$3,140.67
08/15/14	GLAIC payment		$3,140.67
			$37,413.60

Schedule A
Receipts during Period, by Category
Case Number:

Report dates: From 09/01/2013 to 08/31/2014

		Principal Amount	*Non-Principal Amount*

Lump Sum Payments

11/15/13	Lump Sum Payment Per Settlement Agreement		$300,000.00

Sales of Investments

Raymond James
Brokerage Account
Account No:

		No Shs	

Blackrock Floating Rate Income

07/01/14	Sold	1479.739	$15,581.65

Global Long/Short Credit Fund

07/01/14	Sold	1419.694	$15,503.06

GNMA Portfolio

10/01/13	Sold	376.086	$3,659.32

Schedule A
Receipts during Period, by Category
Case Number:

Report dates: From 09/01/2013 to 08/31/2014

			Principal Amount	Non-Principal Amount
10/01/13	Sold	376.086	$3,659.32	
10/01/13	Sold	376.086	$3,659.32	
			$10,977.96	

High Yield Bond

07/01/14	Sold	1958.899	$16,552.70	

Strategic Inc. Opportunities

07/01/14	Sold	3015.859	$31,244.30	

Principal Receipts	$89,859.67	
Non-Principal Receipts		$339,568.70

Schedule B
Gain on the Sale of Assets
Case Number:

Report dates: From 09/01/2013 to 08/31/2014

Investment sales:

Description	Sale Date	Sale Amount	Carry Value	Gain
Raymond James Brokerage Account Account No:				
Blackrock Floating Rate Income				
Sold 1479.739 shares	07/01/14	$15,581.65	$15,447.03	$134.62
Blackrock Global Long/ Short Credit Fund				
Sold 1419.694 shares	07/01/14	$15,503.06	$14,982.06	$521.00
Blackrock High Yield Bond				
Sold 1958.899 shares	07/01/14	$16,552.70	$15,985.91	$566.79
Blackrock Strategic Opportunities Inc.				
Sold 3015.859 shares	07/01/14	$31,244.30	$30,611.23	$633.07
	Total Gain			$1,855.48

Schedule C
Disbursements during Period, by Category
Case Number:

Report dates: From 09/01/2013 to 08/31/2014

Description Date of payment/Check no/Payee/Amount	Principal Amount	Non- Principal Amount
Long-Term Care & Supervision		
09/10/13 1005		$2,276.30
10/07/13 1012		$2,276.30
11/07/13 1021		$2,276.30
12/12/13 1031		$2,276.30
01/07/14 1039		$2,276.30
02/11/14 1047		$2,276.30
03/11/14 1054		$2,492.00
04/08/14 1063		$2,492.00
05/06/14 1069		$2,492.00
06/10/14 1078		$2,492.00
07/08/14 1086		$2,492.00
07/24/14 1092		$2,492.00
		$28,609.80

Payments
to

for SNT Beneficiary
Meals & Entertainment

09/24/13	1009	Trust beneficiary incidentals		$100.00
10/24/13	1016	Trust beneficiary incidentals		$100.00
11/21/13	1028	Trust beneficiary incidentals		$100.00
12/05/13	1029	Christmas		$300.00
12/19/13	1037	Trust beneficiary incidentals		$250.00
01/21/14	1042	Trust beneficiary incidentals		$250.00
01/28/14	1045	Clothes / shoes		$298.23

Schedule C
Disbursements during Period, by Category
Case Number:

Report dates: From 09/01/2013 to 08/31/2014

			Principal Amount	Non-Principal Amount
02/12/14	1049	Mothers Day gift		$100.00
02/19/14	1051	Trust beneficiary incidentals		$250.00
03/18/14	1057	Trust beneficiary incidentals		$250.00
04/15/14	1066	Dryer		$215.79
04/22/14	1067	Trust beneficiary incidentals		$250.00
05/06/14	1068	Mothers Day gift		$100.00
05/20/14	1074	Trust beneficiary incidentals		$250.00
06/10/14	1081	Fathers Day gift		$100.00
06/17/14	1083	Trust beneficiary incidentals		$250.00
07/22/14	1090	Trust beneficiary incidentals		$250.00
07/31/14	1095	Birthday dress		$48.00
08/07/14	1097	Birthday cake		$100.00
08/12/14	1102	Birthday gifts		$100.00
08/19/14	1103	Trust beneficiary incidentals		$250.00
				$3,912.02

Residential Expenses of SNT Beneficiary

Mortgage Payments

09/17/13	1006	CitiMortgage	$1,043.80
10/15/13	1013	CitiMortgage	$1,043.80
11/18/13	1025	CitiMortgage	$1,043.80
12/20/13	1032	CitiMortgage	$1,043.80

Schedule C
Disbursements during Period, by Category
Case Number:

Report dates: From 09/01/2013 to 08/31/2014

			Principal Amount	Non-Principal Amount
01/21/14	1040	CitiMortgage		$1,043.80
02/24/14	1050	CitiMortgage		$1,043.80
03/24/14	1056	CitiMortgage		$1,043.80
04/21/14	1064	CitiMortgage		$1,043.80
05/19/14	1072	CitiMortgage		$1,043.80
06/17/14	1082	CitiMortgage		$1,043.80
07/21/14	1087	CitiMortgage		$1,043.80
08/18/14	1099	CitiMortgage		$1,043.80
				$12,525.60

Property Taxes / Insurance

11/07/13	1022	Don Kent, Riverside County Treasurer		$1,561.81
11/13/13	1023	Sorenson Insurance Services		$1,437.24
12/05/13	1030	US Liability Insurance Co.		$217.00
03/11/14	1055	Don Kent, Riverside County Treasurer		$1,561.81
				$4,777.86

Utilities

10/24/13	1018	Riverside Public Utilities		$496.25

Pool Maintenance

09/17/13	1007	Pool Aide		$100.00
10/17/13	1015	Pool Aide		$100.00

Schedule C
Disbursements during Period, by Category
Case Number:

Report dates: From 09/01/2013 to 08/31/2014

				Principal Amount	Non-Principal Amount
11/13/13	1024	Pool Aide			$100.00
12/12/13	1033	Pool Aide			$100.00
01/14/14	1041	Pool Aide			$100.00
02/11/14	1048	Pool Aide			$100.00
03/11/14	1053	Pool Aide			$100.00
04/15/14	1065	Pool Aide			$100.00
05/1314	1071	Pool Aide			$100.00
06/10/14	1079	Pool Aide			$100.00
07/15/14	1088	Pool Aide			$100.00
08/12/14	1100	Pool Aide			$100.00
					$1,200.00

Pest Control

11/07/13	1020	Terminix			$101.00
02/04/14	1046	Terminix			$101.00
05/13/14	1073	Terminix			$101.00
08/05/14	1096	Terminix			$105.00
					$408.00

Gardener

10/24/13	1017				$160.00
12/19/13	1034				$160.00
02/25/14	1052				$160.00
04/01/14	1060				$60.00
					$540.00

06/17/14	1084				$240.00

Schedule C
Disbursements during Period, by Category
Case Number:

Report dates: From 09/01/2013 to 08/31/2014

				Principal Amount	Non-Principal Amount

Property Management

Date	No.			Principal	Non-Principal
09/24/13	*1008*				$87.50
11/21/13	*1026*				$87.50
11/21/13	*1027*				$87.50
01/07/14	*1038*				$87.50
01/28/14	*1044*				$87.50
03/18/14	*1058*				$87.50
03/25/14	*1059*				$87.50
06/10/14	*1080*				$87.50
07/01/14	*1085*				$87.50
07/29/14	*1093*				$87.50
					$875.00

Property Maintenance / Improvement / Renovation

Date	No.	Payee	Description	Principal	Non-Principal
09/01/13	*1004*	Gerold Construction Inc.	Plumbing repairs		$285.00
09/01/13	*1002*	Preferred Services	AC		$89.00
09/01/13	*1098*	Preferred Services	AC		$385.00
12/19/13	*1035*	One Service Group LLC	Mold inspect.		$385.00
04/02/14	*1061*	Supreme Air Duct	Duct clean.		$125.00
					$1,269.00

Fees Fiduciary and Attorney

Date	No.			Principal	Non-Principal
12/19/13	*1002*				$7,651.25

Schedule C
Disbursements during Period, by Category
Case Number:

Report dates: From 09/01/2013 to 08/31/2014

			Principal Amount	Non-Principal Amount
12/19/13	1103	Albertson & Davidson LLP		$3,329.00
				$10,980.25

General Administration Expenses

Court Costs

10/15/13	1014	RV Superior Court		$465.00
12/19/13	1036	RV Superior Court		$650.00
01/21/14	1043	Bond Services of California		$446.63
06/04/14	1076	Bond Services of California		$1,694.00
				$3,255.63

Professional Services

09/24/13	1011			$682.50

Tax Preparation

04/08/14	1062	Vicente, Lloyd, & Stutzman, LLP		$475.00

Brokerage Advisory Fees

07/16/14		Advisory fees		$42.03

Schedule C
Disbursements during Period, by Category
Case Number:

Report dates: From 09/01/2013 to 08/31/2014

			Principal Amount	Non-Principal Amount
07/16/14		Advisory fees		<u>$773.23</u>
				$815.26

Postage

09/24/13	1010	USPS		$5.60

Living Expenses

Birthday Party (for trust beneficiary)

06/04/14	1077	Marinaj Banquets & Events	Birthday Venue	$500.00
07/15/14	1089	Marinaj Banquets & Events	Birthday Venue	$4,100.00
07/23/14	1091	JBMG Artist Mgmt.	Enter-tainmt.	$400.00
07/31/14	1094		Dress/ Shoes	$302.00
08/12/14	1101		Photog-rapher	<u>$100.00</u>
				$5,402.00

Other Living Expense

11/07/13	1019	VTDM	Church fundraiser ticket	$40.00

Schedule C
Disbursements during Period, by Category
Case Number:

Report dates: From 09/01/2013 to 08/31/2014

			Principal Amount	Non-Principal Amount

Investment Expenses

Raymond James
Brokerage Account
Account No:

	No Shs	

Blackrock Floating Rate Income

Date	Type	No Shs	Principal Amount
09/03/13	Purchased	2.879	$30.00
10/01/13	Purchased	2.800	$29.18
10/01/13	Purchased	350.846	$3,659.32
10/03/13	Purchased	2.230	$23.24
11/01/13	Purchased	3.280	$34.41
12/02/13	Purchased	3.507	$36.79
01/02/14	Purchased	3.341	$35.11
02/03/14	Purchased	3.318	$34.94
03/03/14	Purchased	3.211	$33.75
04/01/14	Purchased	3.519	$36.98
05/01/14	Purchased	3.486	$36.53
06/02/14	Purchased	3.688	$38.80
			$4,029.05

Blackrock Global Long/Short
Credit Fund

Date	Type	No Shs	Principal Amount
09/03/13	Purchased	0.035	$0.37
10/01/13	Purchased	0.068	$0.72

Schedule C
Disbursements during Period, by Category
Case Number:

Report dates: From 09/01/2013 to 08/31/2014

			Principal Amount	Non-Principal Amount
10/01/13	Purchased	345.545	$3,659.32	
11/01/13	Purchased	0.377	$4.02	
12/02/13	Purchased	0.364	$3.89	
01/02/14	Purchased	0.503	$5.40	
02/03/14	Purchased	0.548	$5.88	
03/03/14	Purchased	0.855	$9.27	
04/01/14	Purchased	0.628	$6.80	
05/01/14	Purchased	0.547	$5.94	
06/02/14	Purchased	0.540	$5.87	
			$3,707.48	

Blackrock GNMA Portfolio

09/03/13	Purchased	2.345	$22.51	

Blackrock High Yield Bond

09/03/13	Purchased	6.235	$50.32	
10/01/13	Purchased	5.817	$47.47	
10/01/13	Purchased	447.897	$3,659.32	
11/01/13	Purchased	7.270	$60.27	
12/02/13	Purchased	7.067	$58.73	
12/23/13	Purchased	23.419	$192.27	
12/23/13	Purchased	1.985	$16.30	
01/02/14	Purchased	7.819	$64.27	
02/03/14	Purchased	8.341	$68.73	
03/03/14	Purchased	7.382	$61.79	

Schedule C
Disbursements during Period, by Category
Case Number:

Report dates: From 09/01/2013 to 08/31/2014

			Principal Amount	*Non-Principal Amount*
04/01/14	Purchased	7.837	$65.44	
05/01/14	Purchased	6.549	$54.62	
06/02/14	Purchased	6.721	$56.46	
			$4,455.99	

Blackrock Strategic Inc.
Opportunities

09/03/13	Purchased	2.599	$25.83	
10/01/13	Purchased	2.830	$28.33	
11/01/13	Purchased	2.935	$29.58	
12/02/13	Purchased	2.846	$28.77	
01/02/14	Purchased	2.572	$26.11	
02/03/14	Purchased	2.306	$23.41	
03/03/14	Purchased	3.458	$35.38	
04/01/14	Purchased	3.844	$39.44	
05/01/14	Purchased	4.240	$43.63	
06/02/14	Purchased	4.191	$43.29	
			$323.77	

Dodge & Cox Income

07/16/14	Purchased	2211.752	$30,707.00	

Dodge & Cox Stock Fund

07/17/14	Purchased	123.395	$22,311.00	

Schedule C
Disbursements during Period, by Category
Case Number:

Report dates: From 09/01/2013 to 08/31/2014

			Principal Amount	Non-Principal Amount
DWS Alternative Asset Allocation Fund				
07/16/14	Purchased	1004.218	$9,761.00	
IVY Mid Cap Growth				
07/21/14	Purchased	791.646	$19,522.00	
Lord Abbett Bond Debenture				
07/18/14	Purchased	2675.180	$22,311.00	
Oakmark International				
07/16/14	Purchased	1045.277	$27,918.00	
Pimco Commodity Real Return				
07/16/14	Purchased	1442.414	$8,366.00	
Pimco Total Return				
07/16/14	Purchased	2806.587	$30,676.00	

Schedule C
Disbursements during Period, by Category
Case Number:

Report dates: From 09/01/2013 to 08/31/2014

			Principal Amount	Non-Principal Amount
08/01/14	Purchased	2.955	$32.18 $30,708.18	

Primcap Odyssey Growth

| 07/16/14 | Purchased | 445.487 | $11,185.00 | |

Templeton Global Bond Fund

| 07/18/14 | Purchased | 1677.519 | $22,311.00 | |
| 08/18/14 | Purchased | 4.121 | $54.69 $22,365.69 | |

TFS Market Neutral Fund

| 07/16/14 | Purchased | 632.599 | $9,791.00 | |

Vanguard Dividend Growth

| 07/16/14 | Purchased | 1632.373 | $36,285.00 | |

Vanguard High Yield Corporate

| 07/16/14 | Purchased | 2274.715 | $13,974.00 | |

Schedule C
Disbursements during Period, by Category
Case Number:

Report dates: From 09/01/2013 to 08/31/2014

			Principal Amount	Non-Principal Amount
<u>Vanguard Tax Managed Small Cap</u>				
07/17/14	Purchased	255.146	$11,155.00	
Pre-Need Burial				
10/24/13 *1001*	Homesteaders Pre-Need Burial		$9,604.00	
	Principal Cash Disbursements		<u>$298,502.67</u>	
	Non-Principal Cash Disbursements			<u>$76,509.77</u>

Schedule D
Loss on the Sale of Assets
Case Number:

Report dates: From 09/01/2013 to 08/31/2014

Investment sales:

Description	Sale Date	Sale Amount	Carry Value	Loss
Raymond James Brokerage Account Account No:				
Blackrock GNMA Portfolio				
Sold 1128.258	10/01/13	$10,977.96	$11,424.79	($446.83)
Total Loss				**($446.83)**

Step 4: Don't lose hope.

Don't forget that you are not alone. Beneficiary abuse happens to people in all walks of life and usually occurs when you are already grieving the loss of a family member. Our firm, Albertson & Davidson, LLP, has handled hundreds of cases of trustee abuse, and that is just a small fraction of the cases out there. Through this book you have gained some insight into the rights you have and some of the actions you can take to stand up and fight back for your inheritance. There is hope. You do not have to suffer beneficiary abuse, but you do have to take action. No one else will fight this battle for you. Your legal rights can only be enforced through your choice to take action.

The burden is yours to ask the rights questions, find the right legal help, and stop your beneficiary abuse from continuing. Your fight is not just for you, but for your family, your children, and their future well-being. The time has come to stop being the victim and become the champion of your legal beneficiary rights.

About the Firm

Founded in 2008, Albertson & Davidson, LLP, serves abused beneficiaries who are facing financial battles over trusts, wills, and probate matters. Our team of seven estate attorneys has extensive courtroom experience successfully litigating complex and often emotionally charged legal issues.

At Albertson & Davidson, LLP, we are driven by compassion for our clients. We understand the frustration and panic that sets in when you realize someone has been stealing from your heritance or manipulating a situation for their own financial gain. We know how hot emotions can run and how families can be forever divided in long-running arguments over wills, trusts, and financial elder abuse proceedings.

Our aggressive trust and will trial lawyers have extensive experience navigating sensitive situations and successfully securing the satisfactory outcomes our clients deserve. Our firm is strictly focused on this complex area of law, and our trial attorneys have honed their skills in courtrooms all across California. We stand, we fight, and we win.

With offices in Los Angeles, San Francisco, San Diego County, Orange County, and Silicon Valley, our firm is available to assist clients throughout California. We offer free consultations, and if we can't take your case, we will refer you to someone who can.

If you or a loved one's financial future is on the line, you need to take action now to protect your legal rights. Contact us now to discuss your case and set up a complimentary case evaluation with our team.

Website: www.aldavlaw.com

Email: keith@aldavlaw.com and stewart@aldavlaw.com

Phone: 1–877–632–1738

About the Authors

Keith A. Davidson is managing partner of Albertson & Davidson, LLP. Originally from Denver, Colorado, Keith attended Loyola Law School in Los Angeles, where he served as the Note and Comment Editor for the *Loyola International and Comparative Law Review* before graduating in the top ten percent of his class.

With nearly two decades of experience in California trust, will, estate, and probate litigation, Keith has passionately sought to help clients throughout California resolve their legal problems and enjoys thinking creatively to position cases for success at trial. He also enjoys exploring legal topics through his monthly articles in the firm's trust, estate, and probate litigation blog.

Stewart R. Albertson received his law degree from Loyola University New Orleans School of Law before obtaining an LLM degree in taxation from Georgetown University Law Center in Washington, DC. Prior to attending law school, Stewart served as a paratrooper in the 82nd Airborne Division of the United States Army for two years, and before that was stationed along the DMZ border of North Korea and South Korea for a one-year tour with the Second Infantry Division.

With a focus on energetic and dynamic representation committed to achieving just and fair results for his clients, Stewart has helped the firm's clients obtain over $100 million in verdicts and settlements, including a jury verdict in one San Bernardino wrongful death case for $5.7 million (Sloan v. Redmond).

Made in the USA
Thornton, CO
10/04/24 00:13:52